Early Reader React

In the past, I asked well-known writers to endorse my books. This time, I wanted to hear from everyday readers, people like you, who would approach the book as a personal experience. A selection of 50 poems was sent to a wide assortment of readers interested in spirituality. Here are their reactions.

"A wonderful book to have by bedside"

Really, really, really good. It will be a wonderful book to have by bedside to read a poem every morning to begin the day! Thank you.

Insurance company owner

"A fresh glimpse of wonder, love, peace and refreshment."

I found these short spiritual movements an easy way to start the day; reminding me of the simplicity of being here in the moment with an awareness of God within and in every crevice of the beauty of life I am blessed to experience. Sometimes, it just takes a reminder to get "off the train" for a fresh glimpse of wonder, love, peace and refreshment.

Public Health Nurse

"Takes the concept of God out of the sky and puts Him/Her... in us."

Robinson has written not only a powerful book here but one that any person can read, grow and even change for the better. This book takes the concept of God out of the sky and puts Him/Her right where the concept belongs... in us. A powerful opportunity for all of us.

Pastor

"Moves me from the busied, worried outside world to... peace, beauty and love."

John Robinson's writing moves me from the busied, worried outside world to an inner place of peace, beauty and love. When you read his poetry, it transports you off the page into the magical, mystical, healing space where your soul and God live. I have a few special books I keep at hand for those times I need inspiration or uplifting, I Am God: Wisdom and Revelation from Mystical Consciousness *will join them to be read and re-read. John Robinson is a treasure, following in the footsteps of the great poet, thinker and mystic writer, Kahlil Gibran.*

Website Manager

"... a whole new dimension of myself opened up to me."

The verses are both challenging and inspiring. I found I had to put some boundaries on my critical mind. I needed to expand my consciousness to entertain the possibilities suggested by the verses. When I did so, a whole new dimension of myself opened up to me. I would read two or three before retiring for the night, and go to bed with my soul expanding to a place beyond belief. Thank you, John, for these verses. It takes courage.

College Professor

"... a work I will return to again and again."

The focus of most books is information for the mind. Some books provide inspiration for the heart. A precious few lead to illumination for the soul. I Am God *delivers all three, inviting (and challenging) readers mentally, emotionally, and spiritually to sample the blissful state of mystical consciousness. It is a work I will return to again and again as I progress on my spiritual journey.*

Psychotherapist

"... a subtle entrainment with the mystery beyond the words."

The poems in this collection are echoing opportunities to approach and perhaps cross a threshold between the worlds of time and the timeless. Read slowly and inwardly savored, one may sense a subtle entrainment with the mystery beyond the words.

Computer Programmer

"... witty, wise, bite-sized..."

I savored these witty, wise, bite-sized verses on my ongoing mindfulness journey.

Attorney

"... hidden within our conventional identity is spiritual Wholeness."

Beneath, above, and hidden within our conventional identity is spiritual Wholeness. Where we unite with God. These poems express one soul's experience of this union, encouraging us, in our own unique way, to experience it as well.

Minister

"... so true and beautifully profound!"

The poetry in your book is so insightful and inspiring. I asked my daughter, Beth, for a response and her comments were the following: "The words are so true and beautifully profound! He has inspired my soul!" For me, your beautiful words and thoughts caused me to envision a metaphorical image – each poem a diamond like dewdrop brilliantly shining in the morning sun. I would suspect that your book may become a way to begin each day.

Insurance Company Owner

"These words are powerful."

Dr. Robinson is adept at wiping away the fallacies of the world and replacing them with the ultimate reality. His individual verses quickly point out the human experience which imprisons us. He doesn't stop there. For me it is becoming the clarity of reality we can all achieve.

These words are powerful. They are succinct. It gives me the feeling of a greater healing.

Vocational Rehabilitation Counselor

"Took me to a calm, true, divinely human place."

I read it all with a smile, reloading the smile especially at the end of the shorter ones. Pleasing voice with no hint of spiritual narcissism. Took me to a calm, true, divinely human place. I'm 53, my closest friends are seven years to a decade older, and "Aging into God" was the showstopper. By the time I got there I was with you in real time and imagining reading it to my prayer partner. Even the trials of mind and body bring you closer to the one light.

Minister

"... my Soul's light blazed."

After reading only a few of your poems, my Soul's light blazed. Into poems, I waded, I splashed, I danced. I traversed this treasure of words, magic, mystery, mysticism. I stopped. I had to. The magic mystical mirror reflected much of what I know, what I continue to discover and explore. The reflective brilliance stopped me. I overwhelm myself in that knowing. Reading John's words: We move from small self to cosmic Self to discover the one we have been praying to all our lives is who we already are. Becoming what I have always been, is my deepest mystery, profound joy. Thank you, Dr. John Robinson, for the gift reflected in the clear, ecstatic, direct power of your words. My Heart, Aglow. My Soul, Afire. An invitation to remember, and in the remembering my becoming; I shine!

Minister

"... a joyful awakening to the God shining within."

John Robinson's "Selections from I Am God" ... is a glittering array of poetry, laid out like stars on a celestial chart to lead you further in your exploration of who God is, and who you are. But the goal is not to have just another journey, but to actually reach your destination: a joyful awakening to the God shining within.

Novelist

"Each reading is a meditation..."

Your clarity of "what is" is amazingly beautiful, clear, and accessible. Just DELICIOUS!!! Poems may be a descriptor but they are each more a meditation for me. I am finding that I am not pulled to read them but to be with them. To sit with me. To let them seep in and transport, carry me to that from which they came. Each reading an opportunity to go within and discover the Truth to which it points. I have a felt sense of the "transmission" these words carry from the place of no words as I open to the wisdom contained.

Founder/Director of Software Company

"Quite extraordinary."

I found my breath expanding as I read your words. What a world you reveal... Quite extraordinary.

Chaplain

"His words, way and presence are evidence that he is a trailblazer..."

As a spiritual teacher and radio show host, I have met lots of souls moving toward the Light. However, Mr. Robinson is the Soul at that gate taking tickets to allow others in. Make no mistake, John is a mystic. He has a fire burning in his belly and in his heart to reach the "unreachable." His words, way and presence are evidence that he is a trailblazer, leading the way for others around him so that they may glow with him. John, love your words; for they put me in the space of knowing myself!

Radio Show Host

"These poems are balm for the soul."

You have done it again. You have led us on a divine journey and given us a roadmap to live in the garden. If you keep reading the poems, the invitation is irresistible. He addresses the paradox of the quest for the divine when he proposes that, "The one we have been praying to all our lives is who we already are." These poems are balm for the soul. I am entranced by his invitation to "ease into the sacred waters of God. Learn to swim." Savor these poems.

Psychotherapist

"... made me feel more connected to God... in a very real way."

I really resonated with these poems. They made me feel more connected to God and God's Presence in my life in a very real way... I felt more peace and contentment when I read through them and reflected on them.

Spiritual Blog Editor

"... breathes eternal consciousness into the moment."

A golden poppy, opening its petals to the warming rays of the sun, breathes eternal consciousness into the moment. For mindful readers everywhere, especially those who've had awareness of the broader universe, the sacred, God, and their precious relationships to all, will find solace and inspiration in the poppy and this book by John Robinson.

University Professor, Author

"You have a beautiful voice... inspired poetry."

You have a beautiful voice, and have written inspired poetry. I feel blessed to have shared these with you. You are God, I am God, we all share the experience and good fortune of being God, or a part of God.

Conscious Aging Leader

"These poems are best savored like the best glass of wine..."

Through the decades, Dr. Robinson has helped us look into ourselves and the gifts of the stages of our lives. At age 75 he took another deep step into "walking the talk of his life." The longing for inner meaning is never more acute and the desire to awaken and experience the divine love in our being is never more needed. These poems are best savored like the best glass of wine or finest cup of coffee or tea. Taking each sip mindfully, swirling it around in the recesses of your being, comparing it to other sensory experiences, and noticing the feeling of gratitude for the gift of partaking. The poetry gifts in this book will serve you well as a daily devotion, something to reflect upon before or after meals, or something to remember before falling asleep. It is a companion for those who are truly willing to explore the depth of love that resides within them.

Pastor

"I was transported to... the holy of holies."

They transported, affirmed, invited, pointed to an experience... of seeing, being, experiencing, opening to... all of it – presence, the holy of holies. Reading the poems, my soul was singing... I was transported to the place beyond and yet ever present. Loved the invitations in many of the poems and found myself saying YES! Also appreciated the humor when it was there. I felt joy, peace, awe, profound humility, delight, expansion, recognition, stillness... and love. In a sense I felt in the reading and absorbing, there is nowhere to go – but everywhere to be, everywhere the I am God is.

Conscious Aging Leader

Previous Books

Death of a Hero, Birth of the Soul: Answering the Call of Midlife
1571780432

But Where Is God? Psychotherapy and the Religious Search
1560725046

Ordinary Enlightenment: Experiencing God's Presence
in Everyday Life
0871592614

Finding Heaven Here
1846941566

The Three Secrets of Aging: A Radical Guide
1780990408

Bedtime Stories for Elders: What Fairy Tales Can Teach Us
About the New Aging
1780993539

What Aging Men Want: The Odyssey as a Parable of Male Aging
1780999814

Breakthrough
1785350924

The Divine Human: The Final Transformation of Sacred Aging
1780992365

Mystical Activism: Transforming a World in Crisis
1789044188

Aging with Vision, Hope and Courage in a Time of Crisis
9781789046854

I Am God

Wisdom and Revelation from
Mystical Consciousness

I Am God

Wisdom and Revelation from Mystical Consciousness

John C. Robinson

BOOKS

Winchester, UK
Washington, USA

JOHN HUNT PUBLISHING

First published by O-Books, 2024
O-Books is an imprint of John Hunt Publishing Ltd., 3 East St., Alresford,
Hampshire SO24 9EE, UK
office@jhpbooks.com
www.johnhuntpublishing.com
www.o-books.com

For distributor details and how to order please visit the 'Ordering' section on our website.

ISBN: 978 1 80341 263 4
978 1 80341 264 1 (ebook)
Library of Congress Control Number: 2022911264

A CIP catalogue record for this book is available from the British Library.

Design: Lapiz Digital Services

UK: Printed and bound by CPI Group (UK) Ltd, Croydon, CR0 4YY
Printed in North America by CPI GPS partners

The author of this book does not dispense medical advice or
prescribe the use of any technique as a form of treatment for
physical, emotional, or medical problems without the advice of a
physician, either directly or indirectly. The intent of the author
is only to offer information of a general nature to help you in
your quest for emotional and spiritual well-being. In the event
you use any of the information in this book for yourself, which is
your constitutional right, the author and the publisher assume no
responsibility for your actions.

We operate a distinctive and ethical publishing philosophy in
all areas of our business, from our global network of authors to
production and worldwide distribution.

Table of Contents

Dedication

I first met Laura Grace Weldon several years ago in her role as editor at *Braided Way Magazine*. As synchronicity would have it, she stumbled onto my website one day and asked me to contribute to this beautiful interfaith publication, which quickly became a home for my budding work in mystical activism. On turning 75, however, I felt a compelling need to take a sabbatical from public life for an inward journey into this next, and possibly final, stage of aging. I wanted a chance to live more deeply in the mystical truths I had been writing about for twenty-five years. To my great surprise, I found myself writing mystical poetry. Hundreds of verses flowed from my expanding consciousness, uncovering both a new voice and a new spiritual practice. As synchronicity would next have it, I learned that Laura was also an accomplished poet (named *Ohio Poet of the Year in 2019* and winner of the *Halcyon Poetry Award* in 2020) and I instantly fell in love with her poetry. The synchronicity cycle was completed when, in her gracious and thoughtful way, Laura agreed to edit my own roughhewn poetry. So began the mentoring phase of our friendship. This book would not have been possible without her generous encouragement, remarkable poetic sensibilities, and skillful guidance from start to finish. When she said the material was ready to publish, I took the leap.

Preface

Who Writes This Book?

From the sacred largess of
mystical presence,
I bring gifts from divine consciousness,
one unveiling after another,
in unending joy.
What a mystery,
to be me and not me
at the same time,
and yet this writing faithfully cascades,
an unstoppable waterfall of
insights, realizations, and revelations,
marking the completion of my life's work.

A New World

I left the frenzied world of identity, time, and story,
of achievement and performance.
That world no longer exists for me.
I can be reminded of it,
but like a flash of light on the retina,
the trace rapidly fades and I return again
to the Garden.
Here there is no war, strife, or urgency.
My awareness abides in
silence, stillness, peace, beauty,
and love.
We change the world by waking up.
Will you join me?
And bring someone with you.

Introduction

A Journal of Mystical Consciousness

Mystical consciousness has been my spiritual practice for decades. In an intentional, thought-free state of heightened awareness, I sense God's ambient presence and consciousness, entering a state of divinely-infused unity. Here I find peace, joy, and love. I also receive insights and revelations about God's nature and how our absorption in it transforms our lived experience. The more I capture these moments in words, the more richly textured and profound my experience becomes. In my 75th year, I took a sabbatical from professional activities to deepen this immersion. The book you hold is a product of that year.

What's it like to write in mystical consciousness? Picture an old monk sitting at a table before an ancient, sacred, and softly-glowing manuscript. Judging by his devoted countenance, it is obvious that this manuscript must be handled thoughtfully, gently, reverently. In the shadowy quiet of his hermitage, illuminated by a single candle, the monk merges his consciousness with the all-pervading Presence. Holding a quill pen just dipped in ink, he awaits inspiration for the next line of sacred poetry, a line proffered from the transcendent consciousness now infusing his own. I am like this aging monk. Working alone in a now-hallowed space, I write from the deep sanctity of spirit.

But there is more. When he is finished, the old monk looks out the window into the radiant, dancing beauty of nature, offering a vivid contrast to the rich dark tones of his room. He steps out into the light of Creation. This, too, is part of my practice, for after writing, I venture out with my dog, Oona, into nature's shimmering, now-enchanted wonderland to witness, in spell-binding awe, neighbors' yards overflowing with vibrant colors of the latest rhododendron, hydrangea, and dogwood blossoms, along a road sheltered by tall whispering pines with quivering birches, all highlighted by the sparkling waters of the Puget Sound that surround our island home. Soil, bushes, ferns, and grasses tease me with complex fragrances, luring me further in the mystery of the world. Like the Tarot's Fool, I wave happily at each passing walker, loving everyone I meet. Then, while Oona enjoys a new scent on our path, I stand still, mesmerized before Creation's latest greatest show, with joy swelling my heart. Finally, resting on a bench, I am overcome with gratitude for the generous and sublime gifts of nature's sacred incarnation. I sit enthralled as God becomes the world, immanent, perfect, all-inclusive. Creation transforms into Heaven on Earth and my separate self dissolves into the oneness of being, for I am God, too. In this way, my life begins anew each day. I am ecstatically happy to bring these light-filled revelations, and the great joy of awakening, to you and our troubled world.

The work in this small volume is my legacy from 25 years exploring the relationship of psychology, religion, spirituality, and mysticism to the understanding of self, God and reality. May the insights and revelations in this tiny volume expand your mystical perception and transform your life.

The Mystic's Vision

Some people approach the divine through scripture, others through ideas, beliefs, and intuitions. The mystic seeks direct firsthand experience of the divine to explore its perceptual, emotional, and metaphysical dimensions. For the mystic, the entire universe is conscious and alive, saturated by an all-encompassing and loving Presence. In its sacred and timeless consciousness, God becomes Creation itself. Practicing mystical awareness, we gradually awaken from an ego-driven, patriarchal dream of reality to discover who and where we really are, an experience that is transformational, joyous, and liberating.

How to Read This Book

This book invites you into the mystical realm, an encounter that will transform your consciousness and the world you live in. Here are some ways to enhance your experience.

Read these verses slowly and consciously. Written in mystical consciousness, they carry its spiritual energy in their words and revelations. If you pay close attention, this material will awaken the same states, perceptions, and realizations in you. In the process, you will become a mystic in your own way. Discuss these verses with friends, read them out loud to find new depth of meaning, return to the ones you like best and let them keep working on you, or use selected lines as mantras, prayers, or themes for contemplation or sermons. Be sure to approach the verses with a still and silent mind to allow God's consciousness to permeate yours, letting this little book become a personal workshop for mystical realization.

While some of these realizations may at first surprise or disturb you, don't let skepticism or judgment undermine your awakening. Yes, many of these descriptions are outside conventional beliefs, but they are mystical revelations nonetheless and arise from the same timeless, eternal, universal, and sacred dimension of consciousness available to all of us. The mystics have described this transcendent realm over countless millennia and you can confirm their findings for yourself as you go deeper into its mysteries. Decades from now, when a new kind of spirituality has evolved, these realizations will seem obvious. For now, humanity is still learning how to experience God directly.

Finally, you may notice some repetition in these sacred verses. That's because every topic invariably involves the same mystical perceptions, emotions, and realizations. Repetition is also part of their transformational power that seeds your awakening and keeps mystical consciousness open. This practice is how I stay in God's consciousness and how you can, too.

About the Title and the Word "God"

I want to speak to any concerns you might have about this title. Is it conceit, arrogance, or violation of sacred commandments to say, "I Am God?" Here's my response.

Of course, I alone am not God. That would indeed be colossal egotism. But when the idea of me dissolves in mystical consciousness, what's left is God. The mystics have been telling us this for eons. I am God and so are you.

But here's the main point: It can be difficult to directly experience God if you see yourself as separate, small or inconsequential, and God as distant, judgmental or inscrutable. By being God in the awakened experience of unity, you awaken the full power and possibilities of divine joy, love, compassion, and revelation. Projecting this power somewhere else, on the other hand, leaves you waiting for the divine "other" to act, blocking its flow through you, for the divine other is what you already are! You are the one you have been praying to and waiting for! I believe the "I Am God" realization is critical to the mystical activism that will one day carry humanity into its next stage of spiritual evolution.

One last thing. I could have used other words for God, like Spirit, Beloved, One, Cosmic Consciousness, Mystery, and Higher Power, but when I do, people often say, "Don't you mean God?" But more importantly, each of these words speaks to a facet of the divine, while the term God seems to me to be big enough to hold them all. And, despite its baggage, it has long been the traditional term used by Western Civilization. Be assured, however, its use here is not meant to imply gender, patriarchal authority, or specific religion. And it is definitely not meant to be just an abstract idea. But please feel free to substitute whatever word for God feels most sacred to you.

Welcome to your journey into the "I Am God" experience. May it awaken life-changing mystical consciousness, wisdom and revelation, and bring you safely home.

Chapter 1

Becoming God

God Lives in Your Depths

In the depths of your consciousness,
God waits
for you to discover
your true Self.
This is an actual experience.
You are much more than you think.

One Consciousness

God's consciousness fills the universe.
Everything contains and expresses it.
The world is alive, awake, aware,
loving, and breathtakingly intelligent.
We each share this consciousness
though we wrap it in personal identity and
assume everyone's version is uniquely theirs.
What does this mean?
It means you have direct access to
the consciousness of God.
This realization alone can
begin your awakening.

One Being

The material world is literally the
substance and being of God.
Every nanosecond, divinity births

the world from its own essence,
incarnating a profoundly sacred place.
Look deeply into anything
and you find God.

What God Is

God is not what you think or believe.
Rather than a giant person-like figure,
God is an infinite, intelligent, omnipresent,
energy-consciousness of
love, bliss, and creativity
saturating everything with its essence.
Experiencing God,
we awaken divine love in our own being.
We move from small self to cosmic Self to discover
the one we have been praying to
all our lives is who we already are.

To Be God

To be God, we dissolve
into the state of conscious being
that is God,
but we only discover this Self
in an awareness free of identity,
goals, conditions, and preconceptions.
God is not a person, place, idea, or fantasy,
God is an experience of pure consciousness.
We enter God's consciousness
through our own.

God's Mantras

Realizing God's consciousness is our consciousness
begins a new chapter of spiritual life.
New mantras can help bring this expansion.
In a quiet, wide-awake consciousness,
repeat after me...
"I do not exist."
"I am not this."
"I am God."
Don't argue with these words.
Simply repeat them deliberately, consciously.
Notice what you feel,
how perception changes, and
what surprises you most.
Then go deeper.

Going Deeper

Silently, sincerely,
keep repeating,
"I am God."
"I am God."
"I am God."
Pay close attention to what happens as you
dissolve layers of identity.
Notice a new intensity or clarity of consciousness
expanding around and through you.
Consciousness everywhere.
God's consciousness as your own.
This awakened state will
light the infinite beauty of every little thing,
revealing the sacred perfection of all being.
Now begin your new life.

Priming the Pump

Farmers drill into aquifers for water.
To bring it up, they often need to "prime the pump,"
adding water to remove air
blocking the pumping mechanism.
So too with Spirit.
A vast aquifer of divine consciousness
waits beneath our public selves.
Seeking to awaken the experience of God,
we dive into the sacred depths of being,
unite personal spirit with its source,
and prime the pump with the words,
"I am God"
until the sacred life-giving waters of
love stream through us
into the world.

Becoming More God

No one does this perfectly.
Mystical experiences do not fix
long-standing problems and
no one retires in enlightenment.
But we become more God with every
mystically-amplified moment as
the world brightens in our
transforming consciousness.

The End of Time

Our work for enlightenment goes
until the end of time.
But here's the catch:

Time ends when thought ends.
What's left is the dawning of enlightenment.

Easing into Water

Imagine having never gone swimming.
To prepare for your first swim,
you could read a hundred books about swimming –
styles, strokes, techniques, training, body mechanics,
even the physics of liquids,
but the moment you walk into the water for the first time,
it's not as you thought.
In the shocking perception of buoyancy and wetness,
the mind wakes up to what it's really like.
That's how mystical experience differs from theology.
One is the pure consciousness of divinity,
the other is analysis, belief, and expert opinion.
Theology can provide a road map, but it's not God.
Ease into the sacred waters of God.
Learn to swim.

What to Do When You Don't Know What to Do?

Do nothing.
Stop thinking.
Be still.
Breathe.
Be present.
Intensify awareness.
Enter the radical sensory now.
Explore it with passionate interest.
Discover the mysterious beauty of things close by.
Experience your body as pure sensation.

Feel the joy of God's being as your own being.
Notice love now surging from your depths.
You're on the threshold of Heaven on Earth,
everyday reality transfigured in light,
a love affair with God in Creation.
Secretly invite others to join you.
Be happy.
Love unconditionally.
That's it!

In the "I Am God" State,
my consciousness
is calm, holy, and joyous.
Everywhere I go, my presence says,
"I love you,"
enveloping the world in divinity.
Time is timeless.
All is flow.
Every thing perfect,
just as it is,
and it's all one thing.
Life, too, is different.
No rush, no pressure.
I move slowly, consciously, staying in the present
in a realm growing more magical,
alive, light-filled, enchantingly beautiful,
and mysterious by the second,
calling me into ever-deeper communion.
I, too, am mysterious,
entranced and fascinated
as divine consciousness permeates
my delighted being.

"I Am God" Is Not a New Identity
"I am God" is an experience
of awakened consciousness.
We don't become the all-powerful figure
portrayed in movies, collective beliefs, or religion.
There is no ego-inflation here because
no personal "I" exists to get inflated.
The opposite of heresy,
"I Am God"
is the essence and fulfillment
of incarnation.

What's Under the Mask?
We keep looking underneath the masks we wear
for what we absolutely know exists,
but have forbidden ourselves from finding.
We cannot even whisper its truth.
"I am God.
And so are you."

It's Here Before You Start Thinking
Enter the state of consciousness
that exists before it's
highjacked by words.
That's where you will find God.

The End of the Spiritual Journey
The end of the spiritual journey arrives
when we realize
there is no place else to go,
nothing left to figure out.

Enlightenment happens here and now,
not in an imagined future.
Senses heightened, we penetrate the "isness" of being and
God opens like a flower right where we are.

Unravel
Pull the thread.
Unravel your self.
What's left is God.
PS: Don't start knitting another.

Embrace Divinity
When I say, "I am God,"
I feel love's power erupting inside.
Personal problems disappear like smoke,
divine light shimmers the world, and
Promethean chains restraining my soul
clatter to the ground.
Don't shackle the fiery presence of God
that will one day free humanity.
Embrace your divinity.

Enlightenment Is Already Here
Your enlightenment has always been here.
Trying to find it with more thought, books, or techniques
only solidifies the experience of
a false self seeking enlightenment.
Stop searching. Stop thinking. Stop doing.
Wake up.

God's Kaleidoscope

Change is everywhere in the phenomenal world.
Like looking through a kaleidoscope –
patterns fluctuate constantly,
but not the viewer.
Be the viewer.
Love the beauty and artistry of Creation.
Just don't forget who's looking.

The Solution to Separation

To say, "I am God," is to say,
"I am this."
"I am every part of everything."
The solution to the entire problem of separation
is to experience the unity of divinity.

Nine Realizations of Awakening

1.
I am not who I think I am.
2.
All consciousness is God's consciousness.
3.
All being is God's being.
4.
Conscious being is unity with God.
5.
God rises in the depths of conscious being.
6.
Conscious being creates the Divine Human.
7.
The "I am God" experience leads naturally to sacred action.

8.
Divine consciousness reveals that Heaven on Earth is already
here.
9.
This is the next stage of our spiritual evolution.

Contemplate each realization.
Take all the time you need.
This is the roadmap to your new life.

The Alchemy of Consciousness and Being
Merging consciousness and being
awakens the experience of our own divinity.
The Divine Human is born
in the manger of unity.

To See Me, Be Me
Here's the ultimate riddle:
"I am everyone,
but no one sees me.
Who am I?"
God.
How can this be?
We see what we imagine…
a "homeless person"
"police officer"
"mother"
"clerk"
"student"
"criminal"
"nurse"

While we have a backstory for each, we never
see God behind the masks.
Nor do the figures experience God in themselves.
But wipe clean the "doors of perception,"
remove masks and narratives,
and what a homecoming we would have.
One loving family
awaking from a long nightmare.
What is the moral here?
God replies,
"You must be me to see me."
Awaken divine consciousness and the
face of God will shine in everyone you meet.

Meeting God

When I long to see the face of God,
I look in the mirror
and smile in recognition.

Sacred Waters

As Creator,
I don an iridescent cloak
and become Eden.
As the sentient river of life,
tides, hues, scents,
tastes, sounds, moods,
and countless beings,
flow out of me
and back again.
You have lost touch with the
swirling waters of my eternal Self.

It is time to swim again.
Repeat after me:
I am the living God.
I dwell in all beings.
In me awakens the ecstasy of
song, dance, courting, and creating,
of life, love, and longing,
of earth, wind, and sky,
as I dissolve in the
spirit-filled waters of Creation.

Tadpoles

We are tadpoles in the sparkling waters of divinity
preparing for transformation.

Disappearing

Gazing out the window into an August garden,
absent-mindedly surveying the colorful,
overflowing abundance,
I rest in the peace of now.
I enter stillness.
Words lose their meaning,
tumble into silent nothingness.
The mind settles.
I disappear in the void.
Only a shell remains,
and you,
everywhere,
like air.

Within and Without

To go within yourself is to go
within everything, for
God's within knows no boundaries.
My within includes
Earth, trees, sky, plants, animals, and you.
To go without engages the mind's
penchant for conceptual boundaries,
splitting Creation into endless distinctions.
Failing to experience ourselves
within one another,
each becomes the distrusted other.

A New Path to Enlightenment

Satori is not required for enlightenment.
You need only replace conventional beliefs
with sustained mystical consciousness.
Its revelations will bring quantum leaps in your
understanding and realization of God.

Personal Transformation

is the greatest offering
we can make to the world, for
each awakening ignites
humanity's collective consciousness.
Because all consciousness is one,
change yourself and you change the world.

A Forbidden Practice

"I Am God" is a spiritual mantra
often frowned upon by experts.

To some, it smacks of egotism.
But the ego does not become God,
for in awakening, no separate ego is left
to feel superior or important.
Instead, a marvelous new energy arises
transforming personality, motive, and perception,
transfiguring the world
right where you are.
Everything becomes God.
For those who enter this consciousness,
love becomes the prime mover of existence.

Pebble in a Pond

Saying "I am God" is like dropping a pebble
in a very still pond
and watching the ripples
spread across the surface.
If the pond were infinite consciousness,
divine ripples would reach everyone.
What would happen if we dropped
a love boulder in the pond?
A tsunami of love.

Cleansing Consciousness

No problem,
no effort,
no goal,
no time,
no thought,
no body,
no identity,
no past,

no future,
nowhere to go,
no one to be.
Only God.

Waking Up
Waking up erases
beliefs, goals, purposes, and fantasies.
Like a faulty lens,
thinking distorts perception.
You see only what you expect.
Stop thinking,
look deeply, and
you are transformed
by the experience of what is right here,
for it's all God,
including you.
In this gorgeously elated moment,
spiritual awakening happens,
in a glance, a heartbeat, a single breath.
Each day we stand at the threshold
between illusions
and extraordinary revelations.

The Discovery of Silence
Can we take two minutes and not talk
and see what happens?
What's found in silence is here always,
though we miss it in busyness.
The discovery may happen spontaneously
or with intention, but
suddenly we get it:

God's consciousness is everywhere
and we sense it directly.
And just as suddenly,
everything changes.

God's Instructions
Be still, quiet, patient,
peaceful, motionless, without thought.
Whisper my name.
Experience my presence.
Stay with me
in this ever-new moment and
I will bathe you in my consciousness
that will soon be yours,
in this sea of bliss.

Melting into Love
The mind's self-concept forms a "me"
separate from God.
Enlightenment is said to
dissolve this duality back into divinity.
Here's what actually happens:
sensing God,
divine consciousness expands until
separation melts in the
raging furnace of love-bliss.
Then,
I am you,
we are God,
and the world is one again.

Unity Means Divinity

It's one of the central tenets of mysticism.
Either everything is God or it's not.
But if all is divinity,
how can we experience this directly?
Follow these steps slowly and carefully.

1.

Discard all objections to the idea of pantheism,
for they completely reject God's unity.

2.

Adjust your expectations.
Realize that everything experienced directly
and without thought is God.
Everything!

3.

In a consciousness free of thought,
in a still and quiet moment,
look intensely at everything around you.
Keep looking until perception is
crystal clear and the world appears
vividly beautiful and perfect exactly as it is.
You are witnessing God's being,
including your own body.

4.

Pick a focal point nearby.
Any object will do.
Look at it steadily and, at the same time,
intensify awareness of your own consciousness.
Notice now that consciousness is not just in you,

you are in it. It is awake, aware, and present.
You have found God's consciousness.

5.
Like focusing binoculars, bring
God's being and consciousness together
by experiencing your own conscious being.
Soon you will sense conscious being everywhere.
It's all one thing.
It's all God.
That's unity.

Incarnating God
"I am God"
awakens rivulets of love
that spread through the body,
subtle energies of spirit
transforming the self.
From this re-union
we channel the joy that is in everything.
We incarnate God
and birth our work
in the world.

What If?
What if consciousness was God's love
gently holding everyone?
What if life was God's essence
in all living things?
What if God was our very nature,
the cure for every problem?

What if we knew this in our core?
In mystical consciousness, it's already true.
What if you felt that right now?

You Are the Way
Penetrate your being
and find God.
Each person, place, and thing is the way
because each is God.
Perhaps you learned this idea was sacrilege or profane,
but in truth it's the seminal experience in every religion.
Roaring fires of divine love burn deep in our souls to
consume humankind's unity-splitting identities, beliefs, and
problems.
The transformed being that remains after the burning
embodies this love.
God is the ultimate catalyst of change.
You are that source.

A Mystic's Testimony
One moment of full-blasting love
Can be as powerful as any good works.
This is how we change the world.

The Last Train to Nowhere
We live on a fast-moving train of
plans, schedules, routines, and habits.
The moment we think about our day,
we're on board.
This train never actually goes anywhere,

though it takes on
many passengers and tasks,
fills up the years of our lives, then
drops us off disguised as old people.
But sometimes, along the way, we get off the train
and, startled by beauty,
question the whole routine.
Then we board again and forget.
But try this once in a while:
get off the train,
go outside to
meet a tree or child or breeze.
Ask your soul what it wants most.

What God Wants Us to Know

God wants us to know where we live,
to open our senses to now and this and here,
because wherever we are is God.
Divinity pours through the world
like sunlight through silk.
In this radiant splendor,
why would we go anywhere else?
It's all God –
this grass,
this bench,
this heat,
this bird call,
this blackberry bush,
this water,
this consciousness.
In this consecrated moment,
we are sacred, too.
That's also what God wants us to know.

Realizations from the Presence

Our deepest realizations
come spontaneously in the still, silent,
thought-free consciousness
that is Presence itself,
releasing feelings, intuitions, and insights
entirely different than those sourced from
a distressed or racing mind.
Here we discover what it means to be
Divine Humans in a Divine World.

The Secret of Failure

Like a pyramid scheme,
the ego harbors success fantasies
secretly seeded by desperation and failure.
Beneath its quest for glory and greatness,
the ego stands alone, isolated and empty.
Having abandoned the true self,
its plan is bankrupt.
Yet there is hope built into this tragic flaw.
Inevitable defeat or inevitable success will
one day open our eyes to another path –
the merging of self, soul, God, and community in love.
Our bankruptcy is universal,
always difficult,
but profoundly valuable,
and ultimately healing.

Surrendering the Heroic Quest

Your problems will never end
until you give up the quest to fix them.
Relax.

Quit trying.
The idea of "you" creates
the very problems you struggle with.
Freedom, happiness, and vocation
begin the moment your personal movie ends
and you walk into
the ineffable, all-pervading light of God's presence.
We are not in the world for solutions, riches, or fame,
we are here to awaken the power of love
that fuels Creation.

Don't Question Your Awakening

Don't try to figure this out,
just do it.
Analysis, skepticism, or fear of embarrassment
sever your connection with God and
place you back in the thought prison.
Every question,
every "but,"
every doubt,
restores the illusions of
thought and thinker.
You will never understand awakened consciousness
until you experience it, and that
experience will be different than anything
you can think or imagine.

It's That Simple

In "I am God" consciousness, God looks out my eyes,
joy explodes through every cell in my body.
I love everyone and everything.
In this awakened state, I raise the world's

collective spiritual being.
It's that simple.

The Ultimate Question
One day you will reach a crossroads.
Do you want to experience God
or continue on the spiritual journey?
You have to choose.
The first you can do right now,
the second extends your search indefinitely.
If you think about this too much
the choice is already made.

I Cannot Stop Loving the World
In the "I Am God" state,
I enter my essential nature –
the vast and universal force of love.
It flows up from my core
melting inner rigidities
like ice in love's fire.
I cannot stop loving the world.

The Power of Love
Experiencing "I Am God,"
floodgates open to
the greatest force in the universe –
the living, breathing, sacred power of love.
Animating the entire noetic cosmos,
it is fully replicated in each of us.
Each moment of divine consciousness says,
"I am healing the world with love."

Love's Incarnation
In the mystical consciousness of divinity,
love saturates my being,
spreading through and beyond me.
As sound vibration spreads from
one tuning fork to another,
this love vibrates in others,
even those too crusted over to feel it.
In this consciousness, I serve love's incarnation.

Compassion
Compassion awakens naturally
in the experience of mystical consciousness.
Like light, it touches all
no matter how pained, broken, or cruel.
Perfect and forever, it is without judgment,
caressing each with its gentle love.
It's here now.
As you awaken, hold everything in
God's undivided compassion.
Watch love blossom.

We Are Meant to Share God's Power
We are meant to be
and act as God,
to express God's massive powers of
love,
compassion,
joy,
and creativity,
and use them to serve

each other and Creation.
Despite popular opinion,
these are the only powers
in the sacred universe.

Vanish into God

Melt into God's consciousness
and be the One
loving everything
as you.

The Secret

This.
Here.
Now.
Exactly as it is.
Is it.
Is God.
Is everything you need.
The only obstacle
to knowing this
is you.

Chapter 2

Heaven on Earth

Finding Heaven
The logical brain categorizes the world as objects –
house, tree, rock, car, person.
The mystical brain,
sees the world as subjects,
each mysterious and alive,
conscious and sacred,
all living together in Eden.
We know how
to find Heaven on Earth
but we forget,
and then lose interest.

Dropping the False World
Mystical consciousness
erases conventional beliefs about
who and where I think I am
and the stories I tell about the world.
In "I am God" consciousness,
ideas of "me"
and "my" life
disappear,
replaced by an infinitely fascinating
fairyland of light and beauty,
color and flow,
magically arising as we celebrate
the living divine now of
Heaven on Earth.

Presence
Reality is conscious and alive.
It knows us.
Every tree, plant, rock, and cloud
senses our presence as we walk by and
invites us into the divine world
which is their home,
and ours.

Stepping into the Mystery
Stop thinking.
Stand very still.
Breathe slowly.
Become intensely awake and
aware of your surroundings,
especially the way light and shadow constantly
transform the surfaces of the world.
Examine every little thing.
Now focus consciousness back on itself and
feel God breathing you,
becoming you,
becoming Creation.
Whisper your secret name for God,
and love rushes up from within,
ending all confusion about why you're here.
Enter Heaven here on Earth.
Stay awhile.
Wherever you are,
bathe in
the enchanting mystery of
God's conscious being.

God's Show
Every day God puts on an awesome 4-D show.
Light glancing off water, wind-shaken trees,
the smell of lavender and honeysuckle,
hopscotch and lovers,
crisp tasty apples,
snowy days and fireplaces.
Get a front row seat before
your ticket expires.

All Separate, All One
A single consciousness fills the universe
flowing through what appear to be different forms,
like light through magnificent stained-glass windows,
giving each "thing" its unique qualities –
rose distinct from the swallow,
willow from a butterfly,
rock from a fountain,
but in the end, all one Creation.
Understanding this to be reality,
an amazing opportunity materializes:
intimate relationships with extraordinary beings
all equal, all divine, all different yet one,
and none considered inferior or inanimate.
They become our teachers, friends, guides, and consolers.
The cosmos waits for us to take our place in the
democratic community of conscious sacred beings.

Seeing Eden

1.

Thought cloaks mystical consciousness
with identity, time, and story.
We see only what we think.
Ceasing thought
reveals a naked emperor,
until even the emperor disappears.

2.

Naked awareness is mystical consciousness.
Without thought, we don't know
who we are,
where we are, or
what the world is.
Yet that is the threshold.

3.

In mystical consciousness,
we discover the enchanted land we left in early childhood,
woven of mystery, magic, and myth.
Talking animals,
welcoming trees,
singing streams,
great mountains,
and divinity itself
respond to our presence.
Entering this world,
we share rapture with all Creation.

4.
And here's the point:
only mystery will restore the divine world.
What we think we know is
the emperor's next illusion
cloaking Eden.

Timelessness in Mystical Consciousness
Time slows down and disappears in
the enchantment of mystical consciousness.
People, places, and actions grow more fascinating.
This reality-shifting alteration of time expands the
aperture to eternity.
Notice when this shift happens.
It signals the nearness of Heaven on Earth.

Dancing with God
Every child has danced with God.
Not the God of should or shhhh.
The God of tippy toes and swirling skirts,
rain boots in mud puddles,
infectious giggles and divine silliness.
When did you stop dancing?
Want to dance again?

The Craziness Is Our Own
In spellbound awareness,
Samsara melts into Nirvana,
Revealing the world's craziness as our own.

Celebrate

It doesn't matter what others
do, think, or say.
That is the noise of
busyness and controversy.
We are here to celebrate the
cosmic nature of self and world.
Find the ecstasy of your being.
Everything is
creativity and celebration
from there.

Eternity

Fingers on keyboard.
Wedding ring reflecting ceiling lights.
The whirr of house fan coming on.
I enter stillness and notice
myriad sensations of being:
body in chair,
wrinkled skin,
light reflecting off each thing.
Shiny silver computer
on deep brown desk.
Vase of flowers,
blue, green, and pink,
long stems in clear water.
Rumpled Kleenex.
Everything perfect!
Eyes widen in amazement.
This is it.
The threshold of the divine world.
Oh my God!

It is here!
Again.
Deep breath.
Eternity in
a
simple
act of
radical awe.
Divine life.

The Ultimate Artist

To awaken mystical consciousness,
we must learn to see again...
see without
thought or purpose,
judgment or expectation,
see what's here,
now,
exactly as it is,
each detail perfect and complete,
like a brilliantly realized Rembrandt masterpiece composed of
light, form, color, and depth.
Can you sense its all-pervading holiness?
Look deeply into any part of Creation and
you will find God
creating reality from itself in every moment –
The Ultimate Artist.

Birthing God

God constantly renews the divine world
through our awakened consciousness.
The medium of this blessing is

the mystical brain,
translating perception, emotion, and action
into God.
As we renew ourselves
and our work in mystical consciousness,
we become creators in service to Creation.
Without humanity, the divine world would not exist,
for God's dream is born through
our sacred awareness.

Crossing the Threshold into Heaven on Earth

The present moment is the threshold of Heaven.
The stepping stones leading to this
always-new world are these:
Stop thinking.
Intensify sensation.
See. Touch. Smell. Taste. Listen.
Feel your own being.
Allow ancient sensory perceptions to
awaken the experience of Creation
as divinity itself.
Peace is found here.
Happiness, too.
And Love.
They are fundamental
to the nature of Creation.
There is nowhere else
more sacred than this.

Come to Your Senses

"Come to your senses" is a
secret call to "I Am God" consciousness,

inviting us to leave the head-world of
thought, fantasy, and worry for the
timeless, radically here-and-now reality found
in pure sensory awareness.
Every perception brilliantly clear and sharp,
every detail captivating.
Abruptly departing the mind's parallel universe,
we step carefully into the firsthand experience of
Heaven on Earth.

Invitation to Flow

Flow is an experience of Heaven on Earth.
It happens magically during wide-awake,
thought-free, sensory awareness.
You can find it in gardening, folding clothes,
rocking a baby, or singing to a favorite song.
In flow, we take each moment exactly as it is,
without modifying thought, goal, plan, or judgment.
Focusing on our own physical being,
we surrender to its pure energy
and find ourselves dissolving into fluid,
easy, spontaneous, even dance-like motion
filled with soul.
It just happens,
effortless, timeless, eternal, like a river.
Float in it.
But be alert to the ego's siren call for
control, analysis, impatience,
frustration, self-consciousness, embarrassment,
or simply "getting back to normal."
With a single complaint, we trade enlightenment
for ego, and the prison doors of the mind close again.

Give Up Explaining

The mystical essence of reality,
including us, is existence-consciousness-bliss.
It's the singular nature of God's being in the world
creating Heaven on Earth.
The ego attempts to explain this idea
to stay in charge. It always fails.
Only direct perception of Creation's
sacred beauty and luminosity
confirms this revelation.
Give up explaining.
No one will understand anyway.
Experience Heaven.
That's all the proof you need.

I Hold You

in my gently cupped hands of golden light.
I touch your eyes and
before you shines
the dazzlingly radiant creativity of
a sacred cosmos
and the one blazing light of consciousness
that permeates reality.
Be stunned.
Be ecstatic.
Join me.
Be God.

The Cosmic Artist

I am God.
I paint the world in living colors and

dress in brilliantly-designed fabrics.
I offer resplendent sunsets and sunrises,
endless stars and galaxies,
ravishing mysteries.
I am laughter and wonder.
I am you.
Be me.
Create!

All Sensations Lead to God

It's all God.
Look deeply and silently into anything
and you will find inexhaustible
beauty, holiness, and mystery.
Thought leads to thought,
Sensation leads to God.

Finding Creation in a Hot Parking Lot

I light up my awareness and Heaven appears everywhere.
It's always here, beautiful and vivid.
You can "pave paradise" with your illusions
but it's still the sacred ground of God's being.

A Million Ways to Love the World

Please don't judge others for what they do or don't do.
Please don't criticize others for what they say or don't say.
Judgment and criticism only harm you.
Every stinging remark conceals
the entrance to Heaven on Earth.

The Present Moment
Oh my God!
Beauty in a new emerald-green leaf.
Joy in a squirrel's raucous chatter.
Sunshine warm on my face.
Silent mind and all of this.
Eternity in every moment.

You Are Part of the Miracle
Countless billions of organisms
inhabit the living Earth,
creating,
birthing,
evolving,
all nourished by
the sun's energy,
in a cosmos of
infinite proportions and inexplicable processes,
and we argue about politics?
With a brain as miraculous as the cosmos,
stand still and witness this miracle before your eyes.
Creation is not hard to see.
You are an essential part of it.

Watching the House of Cards Fall
When thought ceases,
the false self and its world drop away,
and the mind's house of cards collapses
to reveal we never left the Garden.
We are divine beings in a divine world
spun of consciousness, joy,
beauty, and love.

In this holy revelation,
we come home
to a place we only thought we'd lost.

It Wasn't God
Actions propelled by
our own
shoulds,
habits,
goals,
plans,
fantasies,
expectations, and
self-directed acts
close the perceptual gates of mystical consciousness
and expel us once again from the Garden.
We were never banished from Eden,
we left of our own accord.

I Am the World
In "I Am God" consciousness,
I love the world as myself for
everything is me.
I become a great fir tree, my nesting birds
singing sublime love songs to Creation.
I am the dark and holy night,
I am God walking in Eden.
This perceptual shift happens each time
I enter mystical consciousness to
wander in Heaven on Earth.
Try it.
Stay as long as you wish.

What Is Your Doubt?
Do these Heavenly descriptions awaken and inspire you?
Can you recall mystical moments from early childhood?
Standing in Creation, you witness divinity all around you.
How did you learn to turn away?
What fear betrays your joy?

I Change the World
Immersed in mystical consciousness,
I change the world by
sanctifying, transforming, and loving
everything I see.
I awaken and the world wakes up around me.
I am what God is.

When I am God, Heaven Shines
As mystical consciousness increases,
so too does my awareness of Heaven on Earth.
The world becomes infinitely more
beautiful, perfect, glorious,
intimate, love-drenched, and sacred –
one hallowed conscious being living us all.
This is how Heaven on Earth is unveiled.
Heaven is God manifested.
Experience God and Heaven shines.

"The Future?"
When did it become real?
When did "The Future" replace
the magic of childhood.
Was it report cards, popularity, and proms?

Or surrendering joyful spontaneity to the endless
responsibilities of
career, family, and finances?
"The Future" now consumes our thinking,
exiling us from Eden.
Yet in truth, time is an illusion of mind,
the imposition of thought on the eternal present.
Once in a while, trade the prison of thought for
timeless moments in Paradise.
What do you have to lose?

Dissolving the Mirage
One day we wake up
and realize what we think of as reality
is a mirage:
dramas projected by the mind onto
the perfection of Creation.
On that day, the chains of illusion begin falling off,
and, in the bliss of divine union,
we uncover the true world
to realize it never left.

Choose Heaven
Be a mystic.
Choose Heaven on Earth.
Befriend the conscious beings known as
plants and animals, rocks and mountains.
Love unconditionally.
Dance with Creation.
Reach for the divine
hidden behind walls of thought.

Transformed perception,
not politics or religious belief,
will be our path home.
Choose Heaven.
Begin healing the world.

Transforming Perception Together

The more we all awaken as God –
each being God and God being each –
the more the everyday world will reveal
its transcendent origin,
nature and perfection,
and guide us in the unfolding of
a new humanity.

Chapter 3

Healing the World

·

Healing
In the world of spirit,
healing is not curing or fixing,
it's restoring our divine nature.
However we may appear to others,
maimed, broken, dismembered, or unimportant,
in "I Am God" consciousness,
we are sacred and incredibly beautiful.
No judgment, no comparisons, no shame,
but joy in becoming the
substance and consciousness of God in the
unification of Heaven and Earth.

How We Evolve
Humanity evolves less by force and argument,
than from embodying the all-pervading love
of the sacred cosmos.
That's what Jesus and Buddha,
Moses and Chief Seattle,
Rumi and Ramana
taught.
Let's become
divine beings living in the fullness of God,
co-creators celebrating an always-new community of love.
As the tyranny of mind gives way to the sacred mystery,
we wake to enchantment and joy,
transforming the world
as we learn to love fully again.

Accessing God's Power

We have direct access to the
powers of God.
Those powers are
love, joy, kindness, compassion, wonder, creativity, and
gratitude,
for they are God.
Leaving doubt behind, these powers grow in us.
We come alive in this Garden of Self
tending the world.

Merge with Me, Change the World

Because all share one consciousness,
divine love dwells in everyone.
Intensify this consciousness in yourself and
love ripples the cosmos.
We are the medium of love's transformation.
Become God,
create waves of love,
change the world.

Mystical Activism

The experience of mystical oneness is itself activism.
When "I" dissolve in the All,
torrents of divine love pour through me
into Creation reaching every corner.
As the poet becomes the poem,
and the lover becomes the beloved,
so too does
the mystic become God,
leavening the world with love.
Do you think me crazy?

Be God and get crazy, too.
When I close my eyes and sense
the silent interior,
I realize it's not "me" in there,
it's God.

We Don't Really "Do" Anything

In "I Am God" consciousness,
things just happen.
Divinity transmutes the self
and lives fill with
spontaneity and wonder,
flow and synchronicity,
the one in the many,
love and compassion,
always perfectly
choreographed by the Creator.
We are not in charge of this
love pageant nor
can we improve it.
Did you ever really
make a decision in your life, or
did things change and you called it a decision?
Let go of the wheel!
Imposing our agendas on Creation is what causes
problems in the first place.
Let the music of the spheres
lead you back to
the Garden.
Rejoin the celebration.

The Origin of Mystical Activism
Because there is only one divine being,
my being is God's being, your being is God's being,
and we all share the one indivisible being,
hence the universal commandment,
"Love thy neighbor as thy self."
In mystical consciousness,
what happens to you is happening to me, too,
so I care for you as myself.
When ideas like "you," "me," "yours" and "mine"
cease cleaving unity,
humanity will love the One as the All,
and we will dance together
in a great cosmic love song.

Being God Is Mystical Activism
Mystical activism is about transforming
self and perception in "I Am God" consciousness.
In this sacred transmutation,
I realize I created all this,
I am all this, and
I can transform it
by intensifying my all-pervading
love throughout Creation.
Sharing this process, we all begin to wake up
and a new family of divine humans
rises from the brokenness of the old world.

Every Being Is God's Being
Only when "I am God"
do I realize that every being is God

and I am every being.
This realization changes
my response to the world's problems.
More than parroting "Namaste," I literally
experience the other as God and
everything around me becomes holy.
Being God opens the heart of mystical activism for
now there are no enemies and no problems,
no hierarchy of differences,
only sacred beings.

The Mystical Core of Activism

The loving activism of
food, medicine, technology, safety, and education
saves lives and comforts the wounded,
but the cause of these problems,
rooted in human illusions,
never changes.
In the experience of divinity,
love's creative energies flood consciousness.
Reverential silence, stillness, and presence
allow these energies to move through us,
awakening the experience of Heaven on Earth and
stirring loving actions big and small.
Mystical activism works in the
pristine and sacred moment of "here and now."
Transforming consciousness, we transform the world itself.

The New Way

"I Am God" is
a revolutionary path of great power –

the power of being God,
a power that cannot be understood
until it is experienced,
a power that all can use to
heal and transform Earth.
Each of us is God within God,
each can bring this awakening to fruition.
As we join one another on this path,
our combined power grows.

Counterfeit Love

Many claim God says this or punishes that,
but the God I know is beyond words,
found in the experience of love's
flow between us.
God-talk without love
is counterfeit.

Reaching Out

Mystics know love is abundant as air.
But sharing love with others is a challenge.
Some, barricaded by beliefs, cannot let it in.
Others strike out, too hurt or angry to receive.
In this conundrum, we best start with small gestures
to affirm love never left,
as we seek to meet the other as self.

Work Where Your Love Flows

Some work in the outer world,
others in the inner.

Because they are one,
neither is superior.
Let love's expression show
in whatever you do.
Work where your love flows.

God and Politics

God is not interested in power,
wealth, or winning.
Divine love rains down on everyone.
Entering God's nature, we act from love.
Worshipping power and wealth, we grow numb.
Anyone using God's name for political purposes
does not understand God.
Love unites lovers on all sides.

Working on Yourself

Mystics tell us that Cosmos and Self are one.
In transmuting self into Self
we bring the experience of the
entire sacred Cosmos into humankind.
God's presence then spreads through
humanity like wind through quaking aspens,
vibrating with the same frequency.
Work on yourself, you wake up others.
Our whole being is primed for enlightenment.

The Energy of Being Is Love

In divine unity, I am one with the One.
Because the energy of being is love,

every loving action affects the whole.
I offer all the love you ever needed.
Be in your being and spread it to others.
Watch transformation happen.

The Architect

Caught in a drama projected onto God's flowing Creation,
we are the architects of the world's unhappiness.
We are the bully, the tyrant, the monster, the greedy.
Recognizing this tragic farce,
let us awaken from our collective dream.
When the thought-world ceases,
we see each other's divinity
and discover a world of love.

Saving the World

Some say saving one life is equivalent to
saving an entire universe,
and I agree.
But to me, the world is
already perfect and holy, we just don't see it.
Real reform comes with transformed consciousness.
Our ultimate work as activists is to wake up.

The Greatest Power of All

When I say I am God,
I harness the greatest power of all:
Love.

Prophet, Bodhisattva, or Buddha
In addressing humanity's dream of suffering and injustice,
three sacred paths stand before us –
prophet, bodhisattva, or buddha.
A prophet, outraged at violence to the sacred dream, acts
powerfully
to improve humanity's conditions.
A bodhisattva, nearly realized, remains in the dream
to help others awaken.
And a buddha, fully awakened,
dwells in the pure state of Sunyata,
seeing through the insubstantial nature of all dreams.
Each is a valid state of consciousness.
Each a profound service to the world.
Go where your spirit calls.

Facing Loss
When the heart breaks
and confidence in the future crumbles,
we are left alone in the shattered moment with God.
But, if we try, we can feel holiness surrounding us,
gently caressing body and soul.
Collapsed in sacred embrace,
we breathe deeply,
inhaling spirit
until, recovering our energy,
we rise and go into the day,
fire rekindled until the next shock
calls us back into the mystical presence.
Again and again we learn that
God is more available, and known more deeply,
in defeat than victory.

God's Heart Current
A current of light
electrifies the heart
day and night
regulating rate and rhythm.
But it's much more.
Light suffusing Creation is
the same light that creates the sacred heart of
compassion in the awakened one.
It all leads back to love.

Healing in the Light Body of God
Visualize yourself as the light body of God.
It is the most powerful reality you can come from
to support and heal others.
Imagine holding the other in sacred embrace.
Bring them inside your light body.
In your mind's eye,
picture them absorbing the light of God.
Intensify the image and experience.
Pour in light energy until their
light body glows brightly.
Be patient, no hurry.
In the mystical dimension,
visualization is creation and
taking someone into your divinity
makes them divine, too.
Divinity heals.

Spiritual Perception

Psychics, mediums, and mystics view
imagination as the royal road to
the transcendent realm.
We receive images of departed loved ones
in dreams and when we picture their new activities.
These images are a form of spiritual perception.
In awakened imagination, we can converse with those beyond
the veil,
catch up and share our lives.
Modernity's resistance to relationships
with the departed is tragic.
We're missing loving connection.
Keep the lines open.
Our work as mystics is to bring
Heaven and Earth together.
The first step is reaching out.

God on Self-Healing

I am God.
I heal you with hallowed
light flowing in from
your own divine center.
Bring your broken self to me
with all its complaints.
You need only ask,
in deeply sacred stillness,
and I will make you
a figure of divine light.
Are you ready?
Invite the light in and

begin repeating,
"I am the light body of God."
Feel my light infusing your being
When you're ready, you can move into life.
Your body glowing.
Your mind divine.
Your spirit surging.
Now be me.

Relationships Across the Veil

The loss of a loved one
shatters life, breaks the heart, crushes the spirit.
But truth, purpose, and path hide in the passing.
One truth – past, present, and future
disappear in mystical consciousness.
Your loved one's presence is continuous,
often closer than before,
only the physical form is gone.
One purpose – loss expands your spiritual reality.
Heaven and Earth coexist,
separated only by thought and the dream you live.
One path – mystics view imagination as a
medium of connection across the veil,
transcending all barriers.
In mystical consciousness,
sense your loved one's presence.
Imagine conversing with them and
what each would say to the other.
Stay involved in the relationship.
God holds the door open.
The relationship is not over.

Love's Body

The deeper love's bond, the deeper
the pain of loss.
Whether from death, abandonment,
betrayal, or abuse,
grief surges in the body,
at times unstoppable.
Yet the body incarnates God's bliss-filled nature.
How to reconcile this contradiction?
You are not this dream of loss.
You are God watching you suffer
from a story you keep repeating.
One day, you will step out of your dream into Creation
to inhabit a body of love, joy, and wonder.
Perhaps one purpose of pain in this lifetime is
transcending the dream.
Was that part of your plan?

The Poverty of Spirit and the Spirit of Poverty

When the false self is successful, we lack true spirit.
We practice feel-good spirituality.
When people, finances, or health fail,
we are offered the spirit of poverty.
Poor in material wealth, but
rich in spiritual possibilities,
it is the final gift of tragedy.

Going Within

Every time I enter the Presence,
a huge joyful smile fills my interior.
I am free again.

I laugh out loud at the foolishness of my problems,
and surrender in the arms of the Self that I am,
full of love.

Releasing the Self-Contraction

You know that fear contraction in your body.
The one that's held you in its iron grip all your life.
But did you know this contraction,
which creates the illusion of a separate self,
is also made of God?
In mystical consciousness, feel its painful twisted being
melt back into the bliss of God's being.
It stops contracting, relaxes, and the self disappears.
Careful attention in that
spacious grace-filled moment will find
joy rising from your depths.
It was always there.
Release the fist-like grip on yourself,
welcome your true nature.

The Sacred Wound

We live in a world of false selves,
each with an identity,
role in society,
inherited beliefs,
and imagined security.
Underneath this world,
the disenfranchised
are noticed but never included.
Our defenses are hard-hearted
and spiritually thin.
But one day, security ends.

Age, loss, failure, sickness, or financial hardship
reveal its lie.
We become the poor,
disenfranchised,
broken,
untouchable,
and needy.
As God's woundings
crack our once-impenetrable defenses,
spirit rushes in,
grace appears, and
we wake to an irrepressible love.

Alchemical Fires

Some transformations are created
through anguish.
You break.
But each time,
you are restored,
though not to the
same person you were.
There is purpose in
the alchemical fires of loss.
They burn away attachments.
What does the burning is God.
What's left is a chastened and wiser soul in
deeper communion with the sacred.
Spiritual transformation continues throughout life
as God continuously burnishes our being
until there is nothing left but love's shining.

God Doesn't Accept Your Self-Hatred

Rage is the expression of old pain
lodged in self-hatred.
Only love can soothe that wound.
Open the inner door, find a way
to let love through.
You are always welcome in
the community of lovers.

The Exhaustion of the Old Self

You struggle because you think you have to be your familiar
self,
the one with all those familiar problems.
It's stressful and exhausting.
Let go. I will carry you. I am you.
I am never tired.
I will renew your hope, energy and clarity.
Happiness and connection,
love and play,
will lift you out of bed every morning
to create a new world.
Be me. It's so much easier.

Disruptive Change

is often the
surprising cure to problems.
Breaking the unseen prison bars of
identity, attachment, and belief,
may be a roller coaster but its
destination is freedom.

What does all this mean?
Love everything.
Trust everything.
It's all God.
Do what you must but don't misread
the ride.
What's happening is sacred.

Transcending Suffering with Joy

In times of distress, intense emotions
arise from the body-mind.
But in mystical consciousness,
distress is a TV program
I no longer watch.
Love so consumes my consciousness
that the old "me" is irrelevant.
I am immersed in the joy of loving all that is.

God's Message to You

I am your power to heal the world.
You have handcuffed me too long with your beliefs,
but I am rising inside you now even as you read these words.
Can you feel me saturating your being with love?
Know this: You are a prophet of the new consciousness.
You already have a vision of the possible and
are more powerful than you can possibly imagine.
Find me.
Live me.
Speak as me.
And I will set you free.

Until Now
If I am God, then I am everywhere.
I transform humanity with
joy, love, creativity, compassion, and awakening.
To hasten this new era, everyone needs to be God.
Cradle every crisis in a manger of love.
We are how spiritual evolution happens,
which is why it has been so slow,
until now.

Sadly,
in suffering,
we identify only with the shell
that must crack and break to
release the Self.

The Reward Is Joy
When consciousness merges with being,
love explodes inside and
we are propelled into
the flow of divine life,
moved to listen, love, and act,
caring for the world
with the gifts we
were given to share.
Our reward is joy.

Who Practices Mystical Activism?
Who practices mystical activism?
God!

As the divine presence flows into human consciousness,
"I Am God" becomes spiritual practice and
the source of all action.
Mystical activism is God acting.

The Cost of Resisting

People who refuse the "I Am God" experience
miss the greatest source of healing
in the universe,
because it is the universe.
Fuse "I am God" with "We are God"
and love's fire will
unite the human heart and
light our way home.

Transcending Conflict

An argument begins –
bickering, interruptions, anger.
In the "I Am God" state,
"I" am no longer in the argument.
This is an amazing discovery!
In mystical consciousness,
we transcend the futility of conflict,
and birth a new freedom.

Sanctifying Life

Every positive thing we do
contributes to the evolution of the divine milieu,
but every positive thing we do in mystical consciousness
contributes more,

because in mystically-conscious action,
we are the divine in action.
Even routine activities,
performed in
God's consciousness,
sanctify our lives and
awaken humanity to love.

It's Up to Us
You cannot understand
mystical activism
until you experience it,
and no amount of arguing
will prove or disprove its truths.
Lay aside debate and begin to experiment with
your own mystical responses to life's problems.
Healing the world requires the birth of divine consciousness,
silencing the foolishness of competing narratives and
unveiling the divinity of Heaven all around us.
We are the solution.
It's up to you.
To me.
To us.

The Ultimate Activism Is Divine Consciousness
The experience of divine consciousness spreads
more peace, unity, and enlightenment than
any webinar, book, or political demonstration.
Its power quickens the birth of
human divinity
and the realization of

Heaven on Earth
prophesized in every religion.
But don't believe me,
discover it for yourself.

You Don't Have to Fix Everything
You don't have to fix everything,
you just have to love.
Love completely,
fully,
unabashedly,
unselfconsciously,
and joyfully
wherever you are.
This is your nature as God.
This is your work.

Don't Wait
Everyone pretends to be someone
pursuing important goals or fighting for change.
Break the mirror of self-fascination.
Identity and its grand goals are a prisoner's chains.
Instead, be a mystic, come alive.
Dance.
Love.
Be.
Create.
Every situation is a celebration of God.
Don't wait.

We Are the Problem
Existence is all one thing but
the mind makes it into many things,
this and that,
you and me,
us and them,
human and animal,
woman and man,
God and me.
Struggling in quicksand never works.
Simply put, we are the problem, all of us,
identifying as separate beings.
Move from the many to the one and
know all are God.
Then there is no "other" left to fight.

The Ultimate Spiritual Task
Now I know what I must do.
Inside me resides the power
to awaken humanity to the sacred cosmos.
The source of this power lies at the center of each of us.
We must act from that source.
I am God.
So are you.
Join me in the Oneness
of love.

A Recipe for Change
Change comes through immersion
in the mystical consciousness of being,
magnifying love's presence and power

throughout the world.
Sense it.
Feel it.
Send it.
Be it.
Drop doing, performing, and convincing.
Center your life in the constant miracle
of being.

How Mystical Activism Works
Much of what stands before us is unreal,
a construct of
concepts, beliefs, worries,
fantasies, fears, desires,
expectations, memories, and goals
organized around a constantly revised
personal narrative called
"The Story of Me."
It all dissolves in mystical consciousness,
revealing instead a world transfigured
in light and love
and infinite possibilities.
This is how mystical activism works.

Finding Your Work
Whatever you find yourself doing most
naturally and spontaneously,
without thought or planning,
embodies the union of consciousness and being.
That is your work,
and the signs of this calling are
love, joy, bliss, kindness, caring, and compassion.

The Wastebasket of Grievances
In God's consciousness,
painful emotional wounds,
past and present,
no longer exist because
you no longer exist.
They belonged to an old story
you kept trying to fix,
crumpled memories in a
wastebasket of grievances.

Childhood Wounds
Old wounds,
like a cold, dark, lonely swamp,
suck you down into memories of
sorrow, grief, and loss.
Psychotherapy helps identify and care for these wounds, but
"I Am God" breaks their spell to
reveal your path into the lit wonder of
Heaven on Earth.

Suffering
Does suffering exist in awakened consciousness?
Erase memories of the past and fantasies of the future,
wake up the radical present, and
suffering vanishes,
replaced by a flowing experience of
energy, awe, beauty, joy, and wonder.
Not easy in times of drama,
but a powerful opportunity for new discoveries.
While we are all still working on
this art of perceptual transformation,

the fact remains,
there is no suffering in the unfiltered experience of Presence.

Helping Others from Mystical Consciousness
To help another,
step into "I Am God" and slowly, intensely,
focus on the person, couple, family, or group.
Picture them clearly.
As God, tune into their experience of subtle being,
love them deeply,
talk to their souls,
send them what they need most,
with lots of reassurance,
for they too are full of God.
Bathe them in divine light,
infuse them with peace, calm, clarity, and grace,
psychically appeal to all who love them,
in this world and the next, to
hold them in sacred embrace until
their God-experience awakens,
becomes creative, and begins to
transform their struggle.
You have so much power.
Sense your own way of doing this.
You can't know the outcome,
but you will see it emerging.
The other will find their own way
onto a path of new energy and vision.

Long Distance Healing
In the "I Am God" state,
we can awaken love's creativity

anywhere any time.
Focus it wherever you wish and
look for indications of
increasing openness,
flexibility,
creativity,
happiness,
forgiveness,
kindness,
peace and
love.
Understand this:
it is sometimes more effective to be God
than to pray to God because
we diminish our power
when we wait for our "idea of God" to act.

Help from the Other Side

We are not alone
and the veil between worlds is thin.
Ancestors, deceased loved ones,
spirit guides, and angels
wait on the other side.
They listen for our call and reach out to us in
dreams, intuitions, imaginary conversations, and
moments of loving presence.
They have much to teach us.
Bring them into your life.
And one more surprising thing –
the help goes both ways.

Healing the World Is So Many Things

In mystical consciousness, healing takes on so many forms,
including...
discovering the power of "I Am God" consciousness,
living in the sacred symphony of flow,
unveiling the divinity of Self and Creation,
releasing the old self in God,
reaching across the veil,
realizing the value of failure,
transcending thought, story, belief, and drama,
doing the work you love,
moving from loss to freedom,
releasing the self-contraction,
sanctifying the world,
sharing mystical consciousness,
recognizing you are the problem and the solution, and
experiencing God's light body to heal self and others.
Finding all this and more is mystical activism.
There is no time for boredom.
I stand in awe at the countless
gifts of divine realization.

Chapter 4

The Coming Apocalypse

It Happens Over and Over

Every time greed, violence, hate, and deceit
possess human consciousness,
rot undermines the social order.
Heaven is lost.
Love is lost.
Ugliness reigns.
The world falls apart.
It's happening now.

Facing Our Apocalypse

We are in trouble:
species extinctions, climate disruption,
dangerous viruses, desperate migrations, and
toxic pollution
threaten life on Earth.
Yet in mystical consciousness,
I abide in a realm of joy.
Here nothing matters but God's consciousness,
God being the world,
God pouring love into Creation.
Am I attempting a spiritual bypass?
Here's one answer:
We protect what we love and hold sacred.
As this apocalyptic time threatens civilization,
mystical consciousness will show us
how to love again.
Each apocalypse offers humanity

.

a new chance.
But you will only understand the gamble
in mystical consciousness.

Something Vast Is Happening

Something vast is happening.
Something immense, mysterious, breath-taking.
The whole cosmos is evolving.
I sense it.
Can you?
A vast presence permeates the universe,
awakening our collective consciousness to the holy.
We are evolving.
Pay attention.
Feel it.
Dissolve in its energies
the way
music dissolves people
on the dance floor.

The Unveiling of God Has Begun

Alive, alert, loving, within and without,
God is everywhere and everything.
There is no place we can go that God is not.
The apocalypse, too, is God.
To survive this reckoning,
watch as divinity unfolds its new Creation
and the path back to Eden.
Long overdue,
the unveiling of God has begun.
When the Earth and her beings are experienced as sacred,
we will behold them with the

exquisite tenderness, patience, and reverence of a lover.
Creation is your Beloved.

The Storm
The storm is coming.
It will be wide and powerful.
Those who stand in awakened awareness
will know how to respond,
as God responds,
with presence, with love.
Let the wind blow through you,
it cannot touch consciousness,
and consciousness is your truest nature.
Look through God's eyes –
a pristine new world is being revealed.

Facing the Coming Existential Crises
What happens when we
face existential crises?
For some, terror turns into
mystical awakening for
they embody the same heightened state.
The outcome depends on whether we stay conscious or
race headlong into dangerous illusions.
In mystical clarity, we find that love intensifies
even as social structures fail.
This free fall into God's consciousness
accelerates our spiritual evolution.
Those who awaken in this transformational experience
allow divine intuition to guide them.
A new human era begins
when we no longer act for rewards and outcomes

but from our divine nature to
love and serve Creation.

Crises: The Face of God

We are, inevitably, called to confront
the great catastrophes in life.
The mystical challenge is to be
so radically present that we
sense God as the crisis itself,
breaking the
fear-strictures of the heart,
allowing the awesome power of
divine transformation to be
God changing us into God.
The mystic
surrenders the ego's agenda and
the inner divine moves
to the fore
to show the way
into the sacred dream.

God Is Born in Apocalyptic Times

As psychic shocks from the apocalypse
light up humanity's mystical consciousness,
we birth God in everything we do.
We are being called to create
a new humanity endowed in
love, sharing, and unity consciousness.
God acts through humanity's
intensifying consciousness.
What can you do?
Wake up.

Practice mystical consciousness.
Embrace transformational times as
spiritual practice.

The End of the World

The world does not end in apocalypse,
it ends in a visionary transformation of consciousness,
lifting the veil on a transcendent realm of
light, beauty, and love.
Mystical consciousness will show you the way.
Awaken in Creation.
Risk everything.
Follow your sacred heart.

The Crisis Before You

This crisis before you is not what you think.
It is not a test.
It is so much bigger.
This crisis is an opportunity to put aside your familiar
complaints and
become God's infinite love and compassion.
It's time to transcend the little self
and be God.
Only then will you drink from the Holy Grail.

The Speed of Awakening

Humanity evolved at the speed of glaciers.
But glaciers are now devolving at the
speed of rising temperatures.
As the apocalypse accelerates,
we must hasten our awakening.

Drop your plans and expectations.
Release whatever dream you are creating.
Humanity's awakening is speeding up, too.
We are unveiling Creation.
Look closely.
It's already here.

Trust Creation

As the climate crisis descends upon you,
don't build fortresses.
Turning on others offers no lasting protection.
The tsunami will wash over everyone.
You may even die.
But there is something even more important right now.
Sit with the Earth.
Be still. Be present.
Observe her seasons and her ways.
Everything appears to die for a new world to bloom.
The old one is passing.
Don't go to war.
Trust Creation.

Chapter 5

Listening to the Soul's Quiet Voice

The Nature of Soul

Soul is not a theological abstraction,
it's the presence of the ageless spiritual self.
Older and wiser than its incarnation as true self,
it stands ready in every moment
to guide our growth through
the seasons and cycles of Earth life.
The soul knows why we came and pushes us to
serve the greater transformation of humanity.
Make friends with your soul.
It's been here before.
It knows the way.

Lending Soul Our Voice

The soul speaks quietly inside but has
no physical voice of its own.
It waits,
sometimes for decades,
for us to listen and lend it our voice
in the stands we take
for love, justice, and awakening.
When we speak as soul,
we speak with
authority and power.

The Soul's Message
I am your higher self.
I am what you could be.
Listen to me.
I bring your future as a divine being.
I am what you already are but don't realize yet.
I know you don't feel ready,
but you are.

Listen to the Guidance of Soul
When you stop censoring
and managing yourself,
the soul's voice can be heard,
sometimes in whispers,
sometimes in shouts.
Let it out of the ego's corral.
As God is our ultimate divinity,
soul guides our progress toward that unity,
manifesting its sacred tasks of awakening,
loving service, and Self-realization.
Discover its urgency in the embers of
your passion.
Ask soul for direction and listen.
Do what you came here to do.

Trading False Self for Soul
We can't fix or please the conventional world
of egos and problems,
but we get addicted to trying.
We fantasize about success, adulation, and popularity,
but grandiosity creates rot and
never leads to the true life.

Soul comes from the other side.
It longs to awaken the world and
your own a divine being.
Welcome soul.
Find its authentic voice.
It will be the one you know is true.

The Soul's Invitation
When soul calls you outside
to dance in the sunshine,
breathe in Earth's loamy scent,
and laugh aloud at hummingbird competitions,
it wants you to become part of
this swirling infinite kaleidoscopic mystery of being,
not stuck in the head-scape of identity.
You stand at the epicenter of the world's transfiguration.
Soul is your guide, muse, teacher, coach, and champion.
Answer its call.

From Constriction to Flow
Concepts and thoughts
lock the mind in rigid forms,
freezing our participation
in the flow of being.
Silencing the brain's chatter,
shed the straitjacket of mind.
Soul, waiting patiently in the wings,
reaches out,
takes your hand,
walks you into Creation,
showing you how to challenge illusion and
find the work you came here to do.

Chapter 6

Aging in Mystical Consciousness

Aging into God's Consciousness
Aging initiates us into God's consciousness.
We steadily surrender everything that defines us –
appearance,
roles,
strength and athleticism,
bodily health,
visibility and importance,
and take on the disguise of an "old" person.
But in the void, we find something else,
a new consciousness and
moments filled with
sacred stillness, presence, and transcendent intuitions.
Not only is this our destination,
it's a gift conscious elders give the world.
Words from this consciousness become
revelation, wisdom, and blessing.

The Next Stage in Aging
The "I Am God" state activates
the next stage of spiritual evolution.
In aging's deep space of sacred consciousness,
we surrender the false self
into the living divine energy of the cosmos,
touching everything,
blessing everyone,
affecting the whole world.

Entering God's
consciousness, love, and creativity,
we don't so much change the world as
join the flow of its love.

Telling the Truth

How do I tell family and friends
I have changed,
that the old me passed away
and a new one seeks only
peace, quiet, and the simplicity of love?
Of course, "I" am still here,
but in a new way.
Images of my aging grandmother,
sitting quietly in the garden,
draw me into the waiting stillness.
I offer my grandchildren
her same unspoken presence,
resting in divine being.

Wisdom

Mystical aging isn't about "wisdom,"
it's about being ever closer to
life's pure experience:
old bodies, slower thoughts,
sunrises and cold winds,
loving touch, timeless moments,
deep breaths, honest conversation,
and the steadily parting veil.
Perhaps that is wisdom.

Aging into God

It happens second by second by second.
The slow blossoming of something radically new
growing in the field of losses.
It's happening right now.
Can you feel it?
Past and future recede
into mystery.
Even the trials of mind and body
bring you closer to the one light
shining through everything.
We don't know what a single thing is
but we find its beauty everywhere along
this second-by-second
path into God.

Simplicity

Old age simplifies life.
Sensory and fresh,
fascinating, timeless, and alive,
we enter a world of dancing branches,
mind-blowing sunsets,
children's laughter,
great storms on the horizon.
A world of wonder and transcendence.
Hard edges and sharp boundaries
soften into quilted beauty.

The Highest State

The outer world of identities and ambitions
loses meaning in the later stages of aging.
The past fades,

health problems multiply,
ambitions falter.
But our deterioration has purpose.
We return to the original consciousness of
early childhood reclaimed with mystical wisdom.
Who I am now is so much larger than the
constricted self of the middle years, and
my role expands toward awakening the world.
"I Am God" may be the highest state of conscious aging.

Love the Children

God awakens love in the hearts of the old
to welcome little children into the world.
Don't explain away this miracle as brain chemistry.
Don't steal our joy.
Or theirs.

Waking from the Dream

In our later years,
we often realize "life is but a dream."
In a movie theater,
we remain mesmerized by images until
the lights come on.
In aging, that light is consciousness.
Surprised and astonished, we see
nothing has really happened.
Now, with perception cleansed, we
watch the dream continue but
no longer take it so seriously.
It is a great freedom.
But since we're still in a dream,
may it be a good one –

a sun-dappled path into Creation,
into friendship,
into love.
It was here all along.

When Death Cracks Open the Door
Aging, too, is part of the dream,
as is death,
when the curtain draws back on the drama of life.
We are not what is happening
but the consciousness in which it appears to happen.
In fact, death only happens in the dream.
When the door cracks open,
an even more sublime dream shimmers
in amazing technicolor.
God's next manifestation awaits.

Second Journeys
Gradually, as we age, we recognize
a second journey waits on the horizon,
a journey beyond this world.
To prepare, we reminisce,
let go,
wrap up affairs, and
say goodbyes,
subtly at first, then more directly.
Sensing a sea change,
we await the ship that will
take us across the great waters.
Light filters through the veil of sky.
We smile, laugh, cry, and trust.

Dissolving into love once again,
we know it will be glorious.

Coming to Death

Terminal illness is a final decree.
Suddenly, you're on a moving escalator
soon to become a roller coaster.
All the unfinished issues,
past and present, come into focus.
You learn to
say goodbye to everyone,
ready yourself to meet the One behind all veils.
For the mystic, preparing for death is the
ultimate challenge of spiritual growth.
It is also a divine marriage and a celebration.
How are you preparing?

Spiritual Questions in Preparing for Death

As death approaches, can you...
Stay conscious, present, and centered?
Resist the hook of catastrophic thinking?
Re-evaluate your beliefs about death to
realize it is not what it appears, but rather
an altered state, a spiritual awakening,
and a glorious adventure?
Continually process the intense emotions
holding you here?
Say goodbye with forgiveness and love?
Understand that pain and suffering help you
release attachments to this world?
Return often to the experience of God for
comfort, inspiration, preparation and awakening?

Maintain the joy of life to the end?
Welcome excitement, even exhilaration, for what lies ahead?
Ask for support and guidance from departed loved ones,
spirit guides, or ancestors?
Envision a new world more beautiful than
anything you could ever imagine?
By struggling with these questions,
you can befriend death in gratitude for life.

Chapter 7

The Dream of Humanity

The Dream of Reality
What is reality if not a dream?
Can you prove it otherwise and not still be in the dream?
I say Heaven on Earth is God's perfect dream of Creation,
divine consciousness materializing as a realm of
enchantment, creativity and love.
But we, like the sorcerer's apprentice,
use his power to produce a second dream,
polluting our consciousness with frenzied dreams of
riches, power, conflict, struggle, and suffering.
The journey of life vacillates between these two "realities."
As we wake up from the second dream, we find, to our
astonishment,
God's original light-filled dreamscape, and remember the
destiny
that called us here.

God's Dream
I am a figure in God's dream.
Animated like everything else by
an infinitely creative dreamer,
life just happens.
Knowing God is the "I Am" in all, I let go.
What a relief!
Yet as God,
I am also the dreamer of the dream,
revealing myself to myself.
Such a beautiful paradox.

You don't have to figure this out, but
as the dream continues, consider
releasing your dream-self for the life
created by the original dreamer.

Child's Play

Believing consciousness
to be our own, we take
the long adventure of life.
Like a child playing with toy figures,
we create an imaginary self and play with it.
Duality is God's way of joining the dream for the
pure experience of joy, pleasure, wonder and creativity.
Sometimes we create nightmares and suffering.
But as my grandmother used to say,
"Life is a schooling of the spirit
from the cradle to the grave."
So, be sure to learn
along the way.

Don't Argue with Your Dream

Life is a dream,
but humanity's version
has become a pernicious spell,
its drama luring us ever more deeply
into its myriad nightmare scenarios.
The more you fight with this dream,
the deeper you get.
Lose yourself in the dream,
and you will lose
consciousness for decades,

and perhaps even your life.
Transcend fight-or-flight impulses.
Watch as God watches.
Wake up and discover God's original dream
waiting all around you.
Come home. Bring others with you.

The Dreamer and the Dream

Two insights:
Just as everything in a dream
is part of the dreamer,
everything in humanity's dream
is me, too, no matter how ugly or evil,
for I am its dreamer.
Parts of the dream may seem separate
from me because I don't
like those parts.
But they are still me.
The greater insight is this:
In awakened consciousness,
I am not this dream at all,
I am God's consciousness watching.
This is liberation and a sacred invitation
into the divine life.

Freedom from the Dream

Whatever is happening,
I am not this dream.
I am the watcher.
I have broken my addiction to humanity's fever dream.
I serve humanity's awakening.

Who Is the "Doer"?
The mind's most compelling illusion is the "doer."
We think we are doing the things we do.
In this mind trick, we dream up
a fictional identity, back story,
and life of constant action.
But who or what is the doer?
On waking, I discover I am God
dreaming myself as the doer all along.
The moral?
Release the doer
into the sublime flow of being.
God's dream will take care of itself.

Dream a New Dream
I am not the
doer,
thinker,
hero,
monster,
lover, or
victim
in this dream.
Avoid attachment to a personal self or story and
Watch the movie projector create new images
every second of the day
in your consciousness.
Then wake up as God dreams
a perfect dream,
and see what changes.

The Dream of Suffering

Pain, cold, hunger, and sickness
arise from the divisive world we create
by misusing God's dream power.
We craft the world's trauma and suffering.
God's dream of Creation is pure holiness,
God as Paradise.
So, look closely at your suffering.
Every situation is different than you think.
How do you add pain and suffering
to God's dream?

Lost in the Wrong Dream Again

Notice the dream you are watching,
but don't get caught in the sorcerer's spell.
That's what happens when you forget you're God.
Practice waking up each day.
Ignore the hundred thousand
veils of illusion and focus steadily on the
confluence of consciousness and being.
As these rivers merge, an irrepressible current of joy
will carry you back into God's
dream of Creation.

Aladdin's Lamp

You use Aladdin's magic lamp
to entrance yourself with wishes,
forget who you really are, and
and fall back into humanity's dream.
The genie is a trickster.
You are the genie.

The Dream Self and the Dream
When a child's emerging self
confronts civilization's impossible contradictions,
a dream of struggle and strife is born.
Transcend the personal dreamer
and the dream disappears.
We solve the world's problems
not by fighting with them
but by waking each day from our own
separate dreams.

A World Awakened in Wonder
Abandoning plans and ambitions brings
the world surprisingly alive.
To the soul intent on awakening,
unexpectedly wonderful perceptions
and soul-ravishing joy
return for possibly
the first time since childhood.
Creation opens her inexhaustible gifts, offering...
the smell of rain,
sound of wind chimes and bird calls,
a dawn of transmuting colors – essence of
peach, apricot and cherry spread across a sky,
doubled in reflections on still waters.
Spell-binding visions of a sacred Earth
magnify the longing for
creativity, friendship and play.
Approach each morning in fresh enchantment,
stepping into a divinely imbued world.
Wrapped in a dreamy presence,
surreal and mesmerizing,
we are back in God's embrace.

With this invitation to mystical intimacy,
we walk hand-in-hand on a path of
raptly-altered consciousness,
ripe with magic, majesty, and mystery,
out of humanity's dream.
We are home.

The Surprise Ending

Your dream is a curriculum you created to awaken.
Be compassionate with it but remember
it's a dream you must release.
God is within you watching this experience,
waiting for the surprise ending.

Chapter 8

Final Revelations

Ultimately, It's All Mystical!

We can look at events through many lenses –
belief, science, religion, and psychology,
but ultimately,
it's all mystical.
In mystical consciousness,
we meet God as reality and encounter
something so beautiful
we fall to our knees.

The Hidden Path

There is a hidden path in an obvious place.
It's always been right here.
Walk it not for fame or riches but for the
sacred transformation of existence.
Reaching its prophesized destination,
we finally understand
the pearl of great price
was always at our feet.

The Possibilities of Sacred Consciousness

We are just beginning to experience the
possibilities of mystical awareness.
Possibilities like...
dissolving the false world,
experiencing awakened consciousness,
realizing Heaven on Earth,

embracing the powers of God,
building sacred community,
becoming divine humans,
communicating across the veil, and
healing the planet.
This new consciousness is
evolution's urgent objective.
It's already here.
You're it.

Nothing to Accomplish

The quest for grandiose achievement
often belies secret fears of
helplessness,
inferiority,
rejection,
and mortality.
Big wins are temporary highs,
never permanently erasing anxiety.
The good news is that
fears die with the false self.
We are God's evolving mystery
and divine revelation,
not a self-improvement project or
contest to win.
Real accomplishments happen when
God's being you.

The End of Questions

We often ask questions like,
"Who am I?"
"Why am I here?"

"What is the meaning of life?"
No other animals ask such questions.
But here's the ultimate answer:
Happiness and enlightenment are found
when we stop asking questions and
return attention to the radical present.
Like flower, orca, and sky,
we fulfill our role in the cosmos
by simply being part of the divinity of
what is.

Freedom to Grow Again
Thought is sticky, addictive, illusory.
It spits out fictions by the nanosecond.
It traps us in imagined dramas
and separates us from God.
When the mind quiets,
God stands before us in
myriad miracles and possibilities
Thought transcended
is freedom to grow again.

Sand in an Hourglass
No one should tell another who they are,
what beliefs they should hold
or whether their work is valuable.
On awakening,
judgment and opinion
fall like sand in an hourglass,
in the empty silence
of thought transcended.

Einstein's Mysticism

We knew he was mystically inclined.
Let's rewrite his famous equation
$$E = mc^2$$
from a mystical perspective.
Translate the word "Energy" as Enlightenment
Read "mc" as mystical consciousness.
What do we get?
Enlightenment = Mystical Consciousness Squared.
Focusing mystical consciousness back on itself
is enlightenment,
for we are looking directly into God.
Another proof of your divinity.

Time and Eternity

In mystical consciousness,
time ceases,
past and future disappear,
clock and calendar lose all relevance.
With no rush, schedule, or deadlines,
we enter the holy mystery
and the patient work of eternity.
What we are becoming has
forever to blossom,
and forever is but a moment.
What touches the eternal lasts,
what lives in time fades in oblivion.
Let your work concern eternity.

The Mystery of Consciousness
Consciousness is ultimately
unfathomable, inexplicable, irreducible,
indestructible, and mysterious.
We will never demote it to brain anatomy, never
capture it in scientific studies or philosophical treatises.
Nor can it be subsumed as something else or
broken into component parts.
It is everywhere we look,
central to our looking,
and the one looking.
We might as well call consciousness God.
Can you think of a better term?
And since consciousness is essential to who we are,
I guess that means
we are God, too.

The Walls of Your Prison
Every belief you have is a prison wall
controlling what you can
experience and understand.
More beliefs will not free you.
Stop thinking and walk out.

We Are God's Creative Mind
The one great mind manifests itself as reality,
evolving and experimenting in ecstatic profusion.
We all share in this mind's vision and power.
Participate. Create. Experiment. Grow.

The Joy You Will Know

Don't make enlightenment an achievement.
It won't make you more important,
it will make you less.
But the joy you will know!

The Great Transformation

God absorbs us in mystical consciousness.
Problems disappear like
fog on a sunny day
until only God is left.
Then someone else comes out of "you"
to live in a new world.
Don't advertise your transformed state,
just be it as you love the world
into divinity.

Becoming the Cosmos

I am the cosmos.
How can it be otherwise?
Lift off the thin veneer of identity and
what's left is God –
the living, divine, conscious immensity of Being.
This is the mystic's spectacular discovery.
Find out for yourself and never go back
to the straitjacket of
who you thought you were in
the marketplace of opinions.

The Cosmic Experience
When we awaken cosmic unity,
we are one with all that is.
Infinity inside and out.
An astonishing feeling!
No place to go that isn't God.
No one to meet that isn't divine.
Floating in divinity,
a different life awaits,
where love abounds and you are it.
Your occupation now is love.

The Music of Divine Being
As different musical instruments
blend into a harmonious whole,
a unique sound and phrasing come from each
contributing the fullness of the composition.
God vibrates the stirs the strings of your being
and a song rises in your soul to offer the whole.
Can you hear it?
You play an essential part in
the great symphony of
Creation.

You're Not in Charge
The world is God happening.
Listen to a stream and follow its advice.
Go deep into the forest and
learn from its consciousness.
Nature is full of voices showing us the way.

You were never in control.
Spirituality is about finding your place
in the sacred dance of Creation.

Where to Find the Solution
The logical mind is enemy of mystical awakening.
On and on we think there is something to do or fix,
think the answer lies somewhere else,
think there are more problems to solve,
yet we have already found the treasure.
I am looking at it right now.

How Often Are You Conscious?
Looking back over your day,
when were you last conscious?
I mean, really conscious,
conscious that you were conscious?
That's the key.
In those moments,
you stand in God's Presence,
and in Eden.

The Doer and the Flow
When I release the personal "me" as doer,
I join the flow of being.
I move slowly, consciously, lightly,
self-aware and aware of Self.
I am a mother gently rocking her baby,
a breeze rustling autumn leaves.

Things happen by themselves.
Supper gets fixed, the diaper changed, the leaves raked.
Calm, contentment, and love unite us in Creation's flow, for
action comes effortlessly when the "doer" is gone.
But in the moment of imagined threat,
unity cracks and crumbles,
fear shatters flow, and
I again become the doer.
Could we learn to live without fear
in sacred consciousness?

Trails of Happiness

Leaving the conventional world does not mean
dropping out of life.
It means being so fully in love that
everything changes.
Transcending rules, boundaries, and barriers,
we move fluidly through the world,
leaving only trails of happiness.

God's Fire

Finding "I Am God" consciousness is like starting a fire with
dry kindling.
Small flames of insight begin, uncertain, tentative, but alive.
Blow softly and more sticks catch fire.
Gradually white-yellow flames expand into
a light so bright all illusions vanish.
Consciousness is God's fire.

The Secret of Saints and Sages
In the "I Am God" state
every step on my path is awash in divine love.
This is the secret of the saints and sages.
They know who they are and the power they have,
blessing everything and everyone.

Waking Up in the Movie
We live in our own ongoing movie,
lost in its plot, characters, conflicts, emotions, and desires.
In awakened consciousness,
we step off the screen
and burst out laughing with amazement.
It was all imagined.
No longer owned by the movie's drama,
how amazing to be so radically free.

The Solution
Love is not outside you, it is your very nature.
You imagined love existed somewhere else,
in somebody else,
and then went off in search of it
through life's long journey.
Love was lost the moment you created
a self-idea separate from God.
In mystical consciousness,
a different voice whispers,
"I am the love you are seeking.
There is no more need to search.
I am you."

Unfinished Work

What I know, I cannot always do.
What I am, I cannot always be.
Where I am, I cannot always stay.
Therein lies the unfinished work of awakening.
No one has gone all the way.
But every realization is one step closer.

The Cure for Unfinished Business

In the end, the only cure
for unfinished business is love.
Love the world.
Love whatever happens.
No matter how disappointed, betrayed, or hurt you feel,
it's never what you think.
Love is the answer,
the revelation,
and the final freedom.

You Are Already There

You are already free!
You can walk out of the thought prison anytime and
unmask the divine as yourself.
This is where you were always heading,
what you always wanted,
who you always were,
and now you know.
There is no one to be,
to suffer,
to hide.
Stop thinking and wake up.

This was always your path,
the path of direct perception,
direct realization,
direct understanding.
Be me and know a
fullness of love and joy beyond
your wildest dreams.

The Power of Being God

A whole lifetime can evaporate
in a split second of "I Am God" consciousness.
Don't try to figure this out, just let it happen:
You don't exist.
You are not this.
You are love –
joyful, infinite, sourced from within.
And when the mind,
by sheer force of habit,
recreates the conventional world,
anxiety, worry, and pain
will remind you of your error
so you can
step back into bliss.

Don't Quit Your Day Job

Mystical insights don't bypass our
responsibility for
work, family, and home,
but it's good to stop
from time to time
and sit quietly in Paradise.

Doing so creates a healthier balance of
love and work,
ego and soul,
sacred and profane,
dream and awakening.
These breaks motivate our spiritual work
of unveiling Eden for
ourselves,
our families,
and the world.

The Cards We Are Dealt
Long ago, outside of time, with divine guidance,
you dealt the cards you would face in life,
each hand a cipher of transformation
made more difficult by your resistance.
Late in life we understand
why these challenges needed to happen.
We reappraise their value
in gratitude.

The Work of Mystical Consciousness
is profound and never ending.
Its aim is to reveal God as Self,
experience Creation,
and initiate a new stage of human's evolution.
Humanity awakens as it expands
its experience and understanding of God.
There is so much more to learn.
All can contribute to this great work.

Fertilizing Creation

Dissolving into God,
I hear plants and animals whisper to each other,
sacred bells ring and echo in wind chimes.
Standing in joyful abundance,
I know that life's highest purpose
may simply be to water and
fertilize the Garden with
love, gratitude, compassion, and wonder.

Soaring in a New World

You and I,
we are lovers.
We are the sun
that shines on all.
We are the light that fills the heavens.
We are the love that from God pours.
Look around,
it's divinity shining,
it's everything
you've ignored.
Spread your wings,
catch the spirit,
lift off the ground,
begin to soar.
Merge with me.
Join in the wonder.
Forget the image you once bore.
We are the one,
we are its grandeur,
every part of life you can explore.
And still we're born

in each new moment,
in each new form
God restores.
And for an instant
we fly as eagles,
we ride the wind,
we become the storm.

Chapter 9

About Me

The Lighthouse Keeper
The conventional world overwhelms me.
Its hurried pace, multitasking distractions,
warrior competition, endless opinions,
and lack of genuine intimacy,
feel like a voracious harvesting machine
grinding everything in its path.
I choose the quiet, simple
life of mystical consciousness.
Like a lighthouse keeper,
I work solo sending light far out
over dark and stormy seas to
bring humanity safely home.

The Change
I can no longer push myself
to serve the will of my own or others' expectations.
The result is always the same:
the tires go flat, the engine dies, the battery quits.
From this great reckoning,
I live in simply.
A fern among the redwoods,
I have rejoined Creation.

Hypnotized
I was hypnotized for the first half of life,
struggling in a dream of abandonment and redemption,
a script I unquestionably took for reality.
Looking back, I see how the
themes, issues, and beliefs of that dream
created my world,
never realizing that others' realities
were categorically different.
In these final years,
My dream fades to near transparency,
revealing God's original dream
of being me.

Why I Write
From a well-to-do family with
abundant privileges,
I saw at an early age that wealth
and personal stories
do not make a family happy.
I write to understand why
God's all-pervading love
and myriad gifts of Creation are
so easily lost to humanity.
We lament, "Why me?" and "Why this?"
but "why" questions only draw us back into the
thought world from which most never escape.
God doesn't cause suffering,
we do it to ourselves with the dire stories we create.
I write to bring humanity home to the
mystical wonder of Being.

My Life as a Hieroglyphic

Late in life, we can look back on our story
as a cryptic hieroglyphic,
seeking to understand why we came,
the purposes that drove our steps and stages, and
what remains to be done.
For years, my hieroglyphic presented a distressing mystery:
I came into the world refusing to master
the everyday skills of living that others took for granted,
cooking, gardening and home repairs,
as if I were afraid of losing myself in minutia.
For many, life skills are sacred, and I honor that,
but for me they were distractions from something developing,
the way a photo appears from a chemical bath,
or a plant is seen to blossom in time-lapse photography.
As I waited, I often felt inadequate, ignorant, and deficient.
I was the young Buddha, others caring for his needs,
while his nature prepared a mystic's awareness
of life's imponderables,
death, suffering, God, and ultimate reality.
I came as an explorer of sacred mysteries,
wandering in the metaphysical dimensions of Earth's
nearly incomprehensible and mysterious existence,
seeking immanence, transcendence, transformation.
I came to open a door to the next world,
to flood human consciousness with Spirit
and expunge the fateful illusions
destroying life on Earth.
I am a revealer, not a warrior,
asking only that others experience what I have,
and reclaim our sacred heritage of a
pantheistic world.

Ecstatic Fire
This writing is like a moth to a flame.
I can't leave the flame alone
even as it consumes the fiction of me.
I live in Joan of Arc's
ecstatic fire.

Spreading Seeds
I feel like a dandelion
whose seeds have been liberated
by the breath of God.
I give myself freely to this scattering of gifts.
They were never mine to keep.

My Practice
I used to write about my problems.
Now I write mystical verses until the problems disappear.
Naturally, the thought maker
sneaks back into my divine home
with a new set of problems.
So, I write more verses.
Best thing I have ever done.

Fanning the Divine Flame
My daily spiritual transmutation passes
through three experiential states:
I am in God's consciousness,
there is only God's consciousness, and
God's consciousness ignites the
love-saturated ecstasy of my being.

Each day I initiate this alchemical sequence.
Each day, the process takes me deeper in God.

Awakened Perception
Everything is amazing in my house.
Towels casually hang on bathroom racks.
A plant's shadow artistically adorns the wall.
Paint glistens on white baseboard.
Every object and room a work of art in mystical consciousness.
How could I ever grow bored in
God's endless miracle.
And then I realize
I am God
Creating
this perfect life.

Wild Contemplation
Chickadees peck in the earth
for seeds dropped by birds
ruling the feeder above.
They see themselves
reflected in the glass door,
never knowing how close I am.
Their world is still wild, sensory, alive.
Mine surrendered its fierceness long ago,
in study and contemplation.
Lost in rapt attention,
the window suddenly disappears.
Awareness moves outside.
In wild contemplation,
I am back in the Garden,

alive and digging.
In spellbound awareness,
Samsara dissolves again in Nirvana,
revealing the world's beauty as my own.

Friends with a Maple

We planted a pigmy maple outside the
sliding glass door.
After struggling the first year, it burst to life with
multiplying branches and handsome wide leaves.
One day, looking out my window,
I realized that most of the other plants in the yard
already had friends,
but this one was reaching out to me,
as welcoming and affectionate
as our dog, Oona.
I feel very tender toward to my new friend.
I love how he hosts the finches and chickadees
that compete at the bird feeder, and
the shade he provides for free.
I named him Sydney.
A rough wooden bench sits in his shadow.
Sydney and I are learning the inter-species
language of love governing Creation.
This Fall, he promised to share his
joy in Autumn colors.

At Peace with Eternity

Sitting on bone white driftwood,
along a windswept spit,
thoughts still, senses sharp,
I cannot tell whether I am body,

tree, pebbles, water, sky,
or simply consciousness.
It matters not.
Enthralled in a
lucid dream of God's incarnation,
Oona and I sit, silent witnesses,
at peace with eternity.

I Bless Myself

I see God's smiling face in wild landscapes and
wind-driven waves racing across the sound,
in the faces of family, friends, and strangers,
in seagulls, shade trees, and Christmas lights in dark nights.
God's smile lights my interior and I
hear divine laughter at my own funny thoughts.
As I finish these verses, I feel God's blessing and approval.
I did the work I came here to do
and became the man I came here to be.
As God, I bless myself in these final years.

I Am Mystery

Let me stay a mystery.
I don't want to be explained.
I seek only to be
the God I am,
the sacred
revealing itself.

Author Biography and Annotated Bibliography

I am a clinical psychologist with a second doctorate in ministry, an ordained interfaith minister, the author of 11 books and numerous articles on the psychology, spirituality and mysticism of the New Aging, and a speaker at Conscious Aging Conferences across the country. I have been following a singular mystical vision for over twenty-five years based on the firsthand experience of the sacred which was humanity's original religion. If we want to understand the divine, and hope to transform our current human crisis, we must return to the mystical consciousness of divine beings in a divine world. Below is a brief tour through my work.

Death of a Hero, Birth of the Soul: Answering the Call of Midlife (1995, 1997)

- The seminal vision for all my work.
- Examines the male midlife passage.
- Describes of the psychological, spiritual and mystical dimensions of the second half of life.
- Introduces to the mystical experience – our original awareness of a living divine reality that underlies all religion.
- Imagines the mystical transformations possible in the second half of life.

But Where Is God? Psychotherapy and the Religious Search (1999)

- Conventional psychotherapy completely misses mystical dimension of healing.

- This book for counseling professionals outlines the responsible integration of psychotherapy and spirituality.
- Presents a profound model of the religious psyche and its spiritual journey.

Ordinary Enlightenment: Experiencing God's Presence in Everyday Life (2000)

- Explores the experience of Presence central to the mystical experience: What it is, how can we experience it, and the many ways it transforms our perception of the world.
- Introduces the practice of Mystical Consciousness awakening the awareness of God's Presence and the perception of Heaven on Earth.

Finding Heaven Here (2009)

- My Doctor of Ministry dissertation.
- Engages a chorus of mystic voices all describing the direct perception of the Heaven on Earth here and now.
- The earlier model of the religious psyche now evolves into a tool for understanding, perceiving, and living in Heaven on Earth (Heaven's Compass).
- Contains exercises for cultivating the mystical experience of Heaven on Earth.

The Three Secrets of Aging (2012)

- Shares my own mystical experience of aging.
- Describes the natural unfolding of mystical consciousness in the aging process.
- Outlines the central dynamics of mystical aging: Aging is an initiation into a new dimension of life, a transformation

of self and consciousness, and a revelation of a sacred world all around us.

Bedtime Stories for Elders: What Fairy Tales Can Teach Us About the New Aging (2012)

- Presents the mystical nature of aging in a fun and symbolic way.
- A collection old and new fairy tales, each an allegory of the transformative dynamics of humanity's new aging.
- Journaling questions and experiential exercises help readers discover the meaning of these tales in their own lives.

What Aging Men Want: The Odyssey as a Parable of Male Aging (2013)

- Introduces *The Odyssey* as a profound myth of male aging (as Bly's *Iron John* did for midlife men).
- Men grow tired of the patriarchal model of compulsive warrior as they age.
- They long to come home to peace, quiet and love, but it's not easy after a lifetime of warrior competition.
- Odysseus' adventures on his ten-year journey home symbolize the tasks men face in opening their hearts and coming home from the war.

Breakthrough (2014)

- Autobiographical novel about a middle-aged psychologist whose life is turned upside down through the mystical experiences of a new client.

- Increasingly affected by this client's altered state of consciousness, the psychologist journeys into the realm of mystical awareness and the revolutionary spirituality of aging, revealing possibilities never before imagined.

The Divine Human (2016)

- Culminates the journey into mystical aging.
- Draws again on the words of the great mystics to describe the coming of a divine human in a divine world.
- Adds my own mystical realizations, exercises for experiencing our personal divinity, and the possibilities of sacred action in healing the world.
- Lifts the veil on a new kind of humanity and new era of spiritual evolution.

Mystical Activism (2020)

- Summarizes all my work in building a new understanding of activism.
- Transforms traditional activism by awakening the perception of sacred reality, which is powerfully motivating – we care for what we love and hold sacred.
- Provides revolutionary new tools for "solving" problems in mystical consciousness.
- Rekindles our relationship with soul and ancestors for their help.
- Allows us to communicate with Creation herself to find out what she really needs.

Aging with Vision, Hope and Courage in a Time of Crisis (2020)

- Acknowledges our global crisis of unprecedented proportions: the COVID-19 pandemic, accelerating climate disruption, uncontrolled population growth, and the consequent unraveling of civilization.
- Argues that seniors are a highly resilient generation with the potential to respond with its characteristic idealism, personal growth, spiritual awareness, and genuine wisdom to this new time.
- Provides both practical guidance for survival and an invitation to reinvent our lives, our work, and our civilization in a new consciousness of Creation.
- Presents an inspiring and timeless parable of the mystical nature of apocalyptic times and the birth of a new human consciousness.

Note to Reader

Thank you for purchasing *I Am God: Wisdom and Revelation from Mystical Consciousness*. My sincere hope is that you receive as much from reading this book as I did in birthing it. Please feel free to add a review to your favorite online site or share with me through my website how the sacred consciousness imbuing these poems resonated with your own spirituality at https://iamgodnet. wordpress.com and https://www.facebook.com/becomingspirit/. May this little volume become a cherished friend and guide.

O-BOOKS

SPIRITUALITY

O is a symbol of the world, of oneness and unity; this eye represents knowledge and insight. We publish titles on general spirituality and living a spiritual life. We aim to inform and help you on your own journey in this life.
If you have enjoyed this book, why not tell other readers by posting a review on your preferred book site?

Recent bestsellers from O-Books are:

Heart of Tantric Sex
Diana Richardson
Revealing Eastern secrets of deep love and intimacy to Western couples.
Paperback: 978-1-90381-637-0 ebook: 978-1-84694-637-0

Crystal Prescriptions
The A-Z guide to over 1,200 symptoms and their healing crystals
Judy Hall
The first in the popular series of eight books, this handy little guide is packed as tight as a pill bottle with crystal remedies for ailments.
Paperback: 978-1-90504-740-6 ebook: 978-1-84694-629-5

Shine On
David Ditchfield and J S Jones
What if the aftereffects of a near-death experience were
undeniable? What if a person could suddenly produce
high-quality paintings of the afterlife, or if they
acquired the ability to compose classical symphonies?
Meet: David Ditchfield.
Paperback: 978-1-78904-365-5 ebook: 978-1-78904-366-2

The Way of Reiki
The Inner Teachings of Mikao Usui
Frans Stiene
The roadmap for deepening your understanding of the
system of Reiki and rediscovering your
True Self.
Paperback: 978-1-78535-665-0 ebook: 978-1-78535-744-2

You Are Not Your Thoughts.
Frances Trussell
The journey to a mindful way of being, for those who want
to truly know the power of mindfulness.
Paperback: 978-1-78535-816-6 ebook: 978-1-78535-817-3

The Mysteries of the Twelfth Astrological House
Fallen Angels
Carmen Turner-Schott, MSW, LISW
Everyone wants to know more about the most misunderstood
house in astrology — the twelfth astrological house.
Paperback: 978-1-78099-343-0 ebook: 978-1-78099-344-7

WhatsApps from Heaven
Louise Hamlin
An account of a bereavement and the extraordinary
signs — including WhatsApps — that a retired
law lecturer received from her deceased husband.
Paperback: 978-1-78904-947-3 ebook: 978-1-78904-948-0

The Holistic Guide to Your Health
& Wellbeing Today
Oliver Rolfe
A holistic guide to improving your complete health,
both inside and out.
Paperback: 978-1-78535-392-5 ebook: 978-1-78535-393-2

Cool Sex
Diana Richardson and Wendy Doeleman
For deeply satisfying sex, the real secret is to reduce the heat,
to cool down. Discover the empowerment and fulfilment
of sex with loving mindfulness.
Paperback: 978-1-78904-351-8 ebook: 978-1-78904-352-5

Creating Real Happiness A to Z
Stephani Grace
Creating Real Happiness A to Z will help you understand
the truth that you are not your ego
(conditioned self).
Paperback: 978-1-78904-951-0 ebook: 978-1-78904-952-7

A Colourful Dose of Optimism

Jules Standish

It's time for us to look on the bright side, by boosting
our mood and lifting our spirit, both in our interiors,
as well as in our closet.

Paperback: 978-1-78904-927-5 ebook: 978-1-78904-928-2

Readers of ebooks can buy or view any of these bestsellers by
clicking on the live link in the title. Most titles are published
in paperback and as an ebook. Paperbacks are available in
traditional bookshops. Both print and ebook formats are
available online.

Find more titles and sign up to our readers' newsletter at
www.o-books.com

Follow O books on Facebook at **O-books**

For video content, author interviews and more, please subscribe to our YouTube channel:

O-BOOKS Presents

Follow us on social media for book news, promotions and more:

Facebook: O-Books

Instagram: @o_books_mbs

Twitter: @obooks

Tik Tok: @ObooksMBS

www.o-books.com